Cy Young

Cy Young

AN AMERICAN
BASEBALL HERO

Scott H. Longert

BIOGRAPHIES FOR YOUNG READERS

Ohio University Press
Athens

Ohio University Press, Athens, Ohio 45701
ohioswallow.com
© 2020 by Scott H. Longert

To obtain permission to quote, reprint, or otherwise reproduce or distribute material from Ohio University Press publications, please contact our rights and permissions department at (740) 593-1154 or (740) 593-4536 (fax).

Printed in the United States of America
Ohio University Press books are printed on acid-free paper ♾ ™

30 29 28 27 26 25 24 23 22 21 20   5 4 3 2 1

Frontispiece: Cy Young, Cleveland Naps, baseball card portrait (1911).
Courtesy Library of Congress

Library of Congress Cataloging-in-Publication Data
Names: Longert, Scott, author. | Ohio University. Press
Title: Cy Young : an American baseball hero / Scott H. Longert.
Other titles: Biographies for young readers.
Description: Athens : Ohio University Press, 2020. | Series: Biographies for Young Readers | Includes webography. | Includes bibliographical references.
Identifiers: LCCN 2020002541 | ISBN 9780821424186 (Hardcover) | ISBN 9780821424193 (Trade Paperback) | ISBN 9780821440841 (PDF)
Subjects: LCSH: Young, Cy, 1867-1955--Juvenile literature. | Pitchers (Baseball)--United States--Biography--Juvenile literature. | Baseball players--United States--Biography--Juvenile literature. | Boston Red Sox (Baseball team)--History--Juvenile literature. | Cleveland Indians (Baseball team)--History--Juvenile literature. | World Series (Baseball)--History--Juvenile literature. | National Baseball Hall of Fame and Museum--Juvenile literature. | Major League Baseball (Organization)--History--Juvenile literature. | Baseball--Ohio--History--Juvenile literature.
Classification: LCC GV865.Y58 L66 2020 | DDC 796.357092 [B]--dc23
LC record available at https://lccn.loc.gov/2020002541

Contents

Author's Note

BASEBALL HAS ALWAYS been a big part of my life, from collecting baseball cards as a small boy to playing Little League and then writing about the men who played the great game so many years ago. When I got the chance to write a biography about the amazing Cy Young, imagine how excited I was! He was the man the Cy Young Award was named for. Each year, one pitcher from the American League and one from the National League win the award, including great stars like Corey Kluber, Justin Verlander, Clayton Kershaw, and Max Scherzer.

I learned quickly that Cy was a good man, a good husband, a loyal friend, and a gentleman both on and off the baseball field. He was not like some of the guys he played against, like Ed Delahanty, who bet on the horse races and visited saloons until the early morning hours, or John McGraw, who would scream at the umpires and break most of the rules on the ballfield. In his time, Cy was one of the most admired men in baseball. A feature article in a sports magazine noted that Cy was unassuming, genial, earnest, had common sense, and was fair to everybody.

Along with being a good man, Cy was one of the finest pitchers baseball has ever seen. He won 511 games, a record that will never be broken. He pitched eleven seasons in the 1890s National League and then another eleven in the new American League from 1901 to 1911. Whatever team he faced in either league, he usually won. Cy pitched against some of the greatest hitters in the game, like Ty Cobb, Nap Lajoie, and Honus Wagner, and beat them. I could not wait to start telling his story.

One of the first things I did was to plan a trip to Newcomerstown, Ohio (near Cy's birthplace), to see the historical society museum, where his memorabilia is kept. My wife and I left Cleveland on a beautiful, sunny, July morning for the ninety-minute car ride. We arrived outside the museum, where a member of the staff had agreed to meet us. Inside, there was a terrific collection of things that were about Cy or that once had belonged to him. Right at the beginning, we saw his favorite chair, the one that stood beside the fireplace at the home where Cy spent the last years of his life. Photos, baseballs, and newspaper articles were everywhere, from his ball-playing days to his retirement years. Even his license plates that read "CY-25" were on display.

After a long tour of the exhibit, we drove on to Peoli, to see the cemetery where Cy and his wife Bobby are buried. The trip took us past some old country roads that Cy had likely traveled more than a hundred years ago. The roads narrowed until we reached the small red-brick church where Cy's funeral services had been held. Behind the church was a gently rising hill, at the top of which stood the fine-looking headstone for Mr. and Mrs. Young. I noticed several baseballs placed there and some coins left behind by recent visitors. Below me were green valleys with trees everywhere, much like the landscape was when Cy lived.

We left the cemetery and started back to Newcomerstown. Before leaving, we drove by the park dedicated to Cy, with a baseball field, of course. On the way back to Cleveland, I thought about the huge impact he had left on his hometown and all across America. I can only hope this biography of Cy Young shares some of that impact.

Cy Young

ONE

IN THE BEGINNING

When I was a boy, I spent most of my time pitching a baseball.

—Cy Young (Cy Young files,
National Baseball Hall of Fame and Museum)

I N APRIL 1865, after four long years of hard fighting, the American Civil War came to an end. Among the thousands of returning soldiers was a young veteran of the Union Army, McKinzie Young Jr., who was making his way back home to Gilmore, Ohio. After spending a few days with family and friends, McKinzie went back to work, helping his father, McKinzie Young Sr., tend to the family farm.

The Youngs had over a hundred acres of land, with cattle, hogs, and crops like corn and soybeans. A one-hundred-acre farm—about the size of seventy-five football fields—was quite large for that time. Father and son had to wake before sunrise to chop wood for the cooking stove, clean the barns, feed the animals, and head out to the fields. They would work all morning, take time off for lunch, and continue through the afternoon until their chores were finished. Then it was time for dinner and an hour or two to relax before bedtime.

The Young family home, probably in the 1880s.
Courtesy of the Newcomerstown Historical Society, Newcomerstown, Ohio

With no more worries about army life, McKinzie married Nancy Miller, who lived on a neighboring farm. Her family had come from Pennsylvania and settled just a short distance from the Youngs. The marriage took place in February 1866, after McKinzie had bought enough land to start a farm of his own. Thirteen months later, on March 29, 1867, the Youngs welcomed a baby boy, whom they named Denton True Young. As an adult he would get the nickname "Cy," but until then, everybody in Gilmore called him Denton or just Dent. A year later, Jesse was born, followed by Alonzo in 1870, Ella in 1872, and Anthony in 1874.

Dent and his siblings had all the time in the world to run and explore their father's land. He had two shepherd-collie dogs who happily followed him around on his adventures. One of the things Dent liked to do most was throw a baseball. As a boy, he could throw a ball farther and faster than anyone his age. Each summer, after school was out, Dent and his friends started to play regular games of baseball. Within a few years, he had become the best player among all his friends and neighbors.

McKinzie Jr. and Nancy Young, about 1900.
Courtesy of the Newcomerstown Historical Society, Newcomerstown, Ohio

Baseball has a long history in the United States, but in the early part of the nineteenth century, the game was played quite differently from the way it is today. There were no **balls** and **strikes,** and the batter could let as many pitches go by as he wanted to before he swung the bat. Pitchers threw the ball underhanded (until the early 1880s), and batters could ask the pitcher to put the ball in a certain place for them to **hit.** If a player wanted to get a runner **out,** he could throw the ball at him instead of throwing to the base. **Fielders** could catch a ball on the first bounce instead of in the air, and the batter would still be called out.

The baseball field Dent played on, and what we use even now, is shaped like a diamond with three bases inside it and a **home plate.** There is an **infield,** the space where the bases are laid out ninety feet apart, and an **outfield,** a large, grassy area that extends beyond the bases. The outfield is divided into left field, center field, and right field. The batter stands next to home plate, facing the pitcher, and tries to hit the baseball inside the diamond.

STRIKES AND BALLS

Strike: When a batter stands ready to hit, you have to picture an imaginary box that is as wide as home plate and as high as the space from the batter's knees to just below his shoulders. This is called the **strike zone.** If the pitcher throws the ball through the strike zone that a batter does not hit or if a batter swings at any pitch and misses, it is called a **strike.** The umpire behind home plate decides whether or not a pitch passes through the strike zone and calls out loudly to let the batter, the pitcher, and the crowd know. If the pitcher throws three strikes that the batter is unable to hit, it is called a **strikeout.** The batter is **out** and has to go sit down.

Ball: If a pitch goes outside the strike zone and the batter does not swing and miss, it is simply called a **ball.** Four balls equal a **walk,** and the batter automatically gets to go to first base—for free, without even getting a hit!

Strike zone.

HITS AND OUTS

Hits: If a batter hits the ball and it lands on the field, he immediately tries to run to first base before any of the players in the field can pick up the ball and throw it to the first baseman. If the ball reaches the base before the runner, he is **out** and has to go sit down. If the batter gets to the base first, he is **safe,** and gets to stay at the base while the next batter takes his turn. The umpire decides whether he is safe or out. If a batter hits the ball a long way, he may try to run all the way to second base or third base—or even all the way to home plate if he dares!

Outs: If the batter hits the ball and it lands on the field, he tries to run to first base. If the ball beats him to the base, he is **out** and has to go sit down. If a fielder manages to catch the ball in the air, before it hits the ground, that also counts as an out. The third way to get an out is by tagging the runner with the ball. If one side makes three outs, that ends their turn, and the other team gets a chance to hit.

In Tuscarawas County, where the Young farm was located, the game began mostly among coal miners and farmers from nearby towns such as New Philadelphia, Dover, Port Washington, Dennison, and Uhrichsville. The men were looking for something fun to do on their day off. They tried baseball and found it to be enjoyable and good exercise; it gave them a few hours to forget about work and just have a good time. Before long, they formed organized teams that played every weekend.

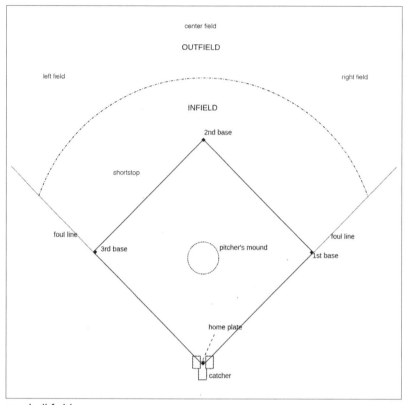

Baseball field.

When Dent was old enough to play ball on the local teams, there were professional teams in the cities of Boston, Chicago, Cincinnati, and Cleveland. The newspapers reported stories about the games and the players. Men, women, and children read the sports pages to keep up with the scores.

Dent and his friends at Pleasant Valley School played in the afternoons, choosing sides and starting a game. Soon the boys complained about Dent's underhand fastball being too hard to hit. After some talking, he agreed not to pitch, but only to play in the infield or outfield. That way, the other team at least had a chance to win.

After Dent finished the sixth grade at Pleasant Valley School, he started working full-time on his father's farm. The property had gotten much bigger, and McKinzie needed his son to help. Like many boys who grew up on farms, Dent had to quit school and work with his father and brothers. Dent was only twelve years old but was already mature for his age and willing to do what was best for his family. The horses, cows, and chickens had to be fed, the wood chopped, and the fields plowed; usually one person could not keep the farm running.

With all that work to do, Dent had little time to have fun. The few hours he had were spent playing catch with other boys or throwing a baseball against his grandfather's barn. When he did not have a ball, he used apples or walnuts to hit a target. Sometimes as neighbors rode by with their horses and buggies, they shook their heads at what Dent was

EARLY BASEBALL RULES CHANGES

In the late 1830s and early 1840s, baseball rules were changed to make the game easier to play. There would be nine men in the field and three outs to each side in an **inning**. All fielders had to throw the ball to a base and not at the runner to get him out. The baseball diamond now had first- and third-base lines to show the difference between a fair and a **foul ball**. By the time Dent and his friends played, the modern rules were in place.

Baseball became popular everywhere in America, from the big cities to small towns. Many men learned the game while they were soldiers in the Civil War. Sometimes when there was no battle in progress and the men were resting, they would choose teams and have a quick ball game. Those soldiers who had not seen baseball before quickly learned how to play. When the war ended, Union and Confederate soldiers went home and taught baseball to their friends and neighbors and in that way spread the game around the country.

doing. They thought he was being silly and wasting his time. He ignored the older people and kept on throwing. Each year he could throw a ball faster, almost as hard as a full-grown adult. Soon everybody in Gilmore could see that Dent had the makings of a real ballplayer.

A few years later, Dent had grown to his adult height of six feet, two inches, the tallest in his family. He weighed around 170 pounds. He could take an axe out to the fields and chop hundreds of pieces of wood. He learned how to carefully split small tree trunks in half to make railings for the wooden fences around the farm. At fifteen years old, Dent could do the work of men twice his age.

At the same time, Dent joined the Gilmore baseball team and began playing other clubs in nearby towns. In one game, Dent and his teammates beat Newcomerstown by the hard-to-believe score of 54–4. Too good a ballplayer for the small-town teams, he soon began playing for larger clubs in Cadiz, Uhrichsville, and Newcomerstown. For pitching a full game, he sometimes got paid one dollar and travel expenses. He was not only the best pitcher in Tuscarawas County, but a fine hitter and fielder too.

When Dent pitched, his club usually won. It did not matter if his town team was playing clubs in a larger city with more men to choose from. Dent would throw his overhand fastball harder than anyone, striking out batters wherever he went. It was awfully hard to beat Dent's team.

In 1885, Dent decided to move west to faraway Nebraska. Why he wanted to leave Gilmore is still a question today. He left his family behind, the people he had been close to all his life. Perhaps he thought he could build a better life there. In the nineteenth century, almost all the farmland from Illinois to New York had already been taken, and it was common for men in their late teens or early twenties to move out west to make a living. People willing to move to territories like North and South Dakota, Wyoming, and Montana or to the state of Nebraska could buy cheap land and build up their own farms. The railroads had expanded all the way across the United States, making it easy for a man such as Dent to buy a railroad ticket and try his luck in a new state or territory.

Dent rode the trains to Webster County, in the south-central part of Nebraska. He settled in Cowles, a small town with a population of several hundred people. He found a job on a nearby farm, earning a small salary and a place to stay. Within a short time, Dent came across the town baseball team. One afternoon, they played against the town of Red Cloud, a much bigger place. Dent pitched a great game, which led to an offer from the owner of his opponents' team to leave Cowles and move to Red Cloud. There he would have a better job and a good team to play for. Dent thought it over and accepted the offer. He traveled to Red Cloud and was given a job at the Ormsby & Dickerson

TOWN BASEBALL

Town baseball was played once a week in many villages and small cities in America. Even if a community had only a few hundred people, all that was needed was nine men who wanted to play ball to make up a team. Each game was a big event with men, women, children, and whole families coming out to the ball field to root for their team. People would bring picnic lunches and buy lemonade and other treats while sitting on the grass outside the foul lines. If a team was playing twenty or thirty miles away, **rooters** might take a train ride to the other town to watch the game. Once the rooters arrived, they would march to the ball field, singing and making noise for the visiting team. There was a great amount of pride in cheering for your team to win. If it did, the rooters could yell and make fun of the losers while the other team left the field quietly. For at least one week, the winning town could brag about its team being the best around.

Two views of Red Cloud, Nebraska, in the early 1900s.
Courtesy of Webster County Historical Society, Red Cloud, Nebraska

Creamery. For thirty-five dollars a month, Dent mowed the large fields and meadows near the **creamery.** The Red Cloud Chiefs were tough to beat when Dent was in the **pitcher's box.**

Living in Red Cloud proved to be a better experience for Cy. The town of nearly one thousand people had five newspapers, three hotels, and two telephone companies. Dent earned a lot more money than in Cowles, had a larger crowd to watch him pitch, and made himself a few friends. Life in Red Cloud was good for him.

When the baseball season ended, Dent found himself out of work. The job at the creamery was there for him only when he pitched for the team. He returned to Cowles, formed his own team the next spring, and did all the pitching. Still, something was missing. Dent made the big decision to leave Nebraska and head back to Ohio and his home in Gilmore. Dent never said why he left Webster County and resumed his chores on his father's farm. When springtime came, he pitched again for several **semipro** teams.

For the next year or two, Dent continued to work on the family farm and play baseball. He pitched for whatever town needed his help and was willing to pay him. He usually won, causing him to be noticed by people all around the state. The people who knew baseball figured that Dent was ready for a bigger challenge. They urged him to try out for a minor league team and earn a real salary. It took some convincing, but in the summer of 1890, Dent got up his courage and rode a train to Canton, Ohio, for a tryout.[1] The manager would decide if he was good enough to join the team.

Dent arrived in his blue overalls and work shoes. Now at about 200 pounds, he looked more like a big farmer than a ballplayer. He threw a few scary fastballs that got by the catcher and slammed into the wooden **grandstand** behind home plate. The players on the field watched as Dent crashed ball after ball into the wooden stands. Either a player or a sportswriter said out loud that the backstop looked like a cyclone had hit it. From that moment on, he was no longer Denton, but "Cyclone" or "Cy" Young.[2] The name stuck for the rest of his life.

DID YOU KNOW?

In the 1870s, organized football and hockey were just beginning, basketball had not yet been invented, and few people played rugby or soccer. If you wanted to play an organized outdoor game between two teams, it had to be baseball.

TWO

THE PRIDE OF THE SPIDERS

The best way to win a ball game is to know what the
batter wants and not give it to him.

—Cy Young (Cy Young files,
National Baseball Hall of Fame and Museum)

C Y AGREED TO pitch for Canton during the spring and summer of 1890. The ball club was a member of the Tri-State League playing teams from Ohio, Pennsylvania, and West Virginia. Each game had only one umpire to cover the entire field. Because of this, there were a lot of arguments between the players and that umpire. He could stand behind home plate and call the balls and strikes or move behind the pitcher's box when a runner was on base. Either way, the umpire did not have a good look at close plays on the bases or balls hit to the outfield.

On April 30, 1890, Cy pitched his first professional game against Wheeling, West Virginia. The other team knew nothing about him. The Wheeling batters did not know that Cy could throw a ball faster than they had ever seen. They soon found out, swinging much too late to hit the ball sharply—or at all.

Even though Cy had never pitched in the Tri-State League before, he did not seem to be nervous. He allowed one run in the first inning, and then one more in the ninth to win the game 4–2. Cy struck out six batters, which was a lot for the 1890s. Outfield fences were a long distance away, and the baseball in those days, usually soft and with little rubber inside, did not travel well. Most hitters did not try for home runs, but just tried to meet the ball and get **singles** and **doubles.** That made it hard to strike anyone out. Cy gave up only three hits, all of them singles. The Wheeling team was able to score twice because of four Canton **errors** and a single walk. Cy's teammates got five hits, two of them doubles and one a **triple.** This was enough for Cy to get his first win as a professional baseball player.

During the season, Cy had some good moments and some bad ones. He was learning to pitch against tough competition. Most of the players were much older than Cy and had years of experience. It did not help that Canton had a bad team that would finish last out of the six ball clubs. Cy managed to win fifteen games while losing the same number.

Soon talk spread around Canton that several professional teams in the National League were looking at Cy and might soon buy his **contract.** The Cincinnati club, for example, had a real interest in him. They already had two pitchers but wanted to add one more. After thinking it over, Cincinnati decided to sign another pitcher, Ed Stein. That gave the Cleveland club a chance.

On July 25, Cy pitched at home against the McKeesport, Pennsylvania, club. He may have known that the Cleveland Spiders were about to make an offer to the Canton owners for his contract. Whether this was true or not, Cy pitched the best game of his brief career. He did not allow a single base hit, recording his first **no-hitter.** He struck out a total of eighteen McKeesport batters, breaking the record for the Tri-State League. The Canton newspaper said of Cy's pitching, "He put the ball over the plate at a speed that would indicate it was fired from a cannon."[1]

Cy's teammates got nine hits, good enough to score four runs. They did not play the field well, making a few errors that led to a single run for McKeesport. Sometime after the game, the Cleveland team paid cash to Canton to buy Cy's contract and offered to pay him seventy-five dollars a month for the rest of the season. This was the most money Cy had ever earned as a ballplayer.

The Spiders were in their second year as members of the National League. Their nickname came either from most of the players being skinny or from the players being too ready to fight on the baseball field. It may have been a little of both.

The city of Cleveland had had several different baseball teams going back to the late 1860s. The Cleveland Forest Citys were the first, then the Cleveland Blues, and then back to the Forest Citys. In 1887, the team played so badly that the owners decided to sell the club to Frank Robison, a wealthy businessman who could afford the cost of making changes. By 1890, Cleveland was still one of the worst clubs in the league, and Mr. Robison was determined to add better players to compete with teams like Brooklyn, Chicago, Philadelphia, Cincinnati, Boston, New York, and Pittsburgh. Mr. Robison had big plans to turn things around. One of his best ideas was to make Cy Young his number-one pitcher.

On August 6, 1890, the Cleveland Spiders picked twenty-three-year-old Cy to start the game against the Chicago Colts. Cy walked to the pitcher's box wearing a uniform that was much too small. The Spiders had few players who were over six feet tall and weighed 200 pounds, so they didn't have a uniform that would fit him properly. The Chicago players started to make fun of Cy's appearance, calling him names like "Farmer" and "Rube," an unkind nickname for people who lived in small, country towns. The Chicago players' name-calling was typical of many baseball players' behavior at the time. They sometimes got into fights right on the field. Cy chose to ignore the Colts and go out and pitch as best he could.

The manager for Chicago was Adrian "Cap" Anson, one of the best players in the National League. Cap played first base and was in charge of the club. He had begun his career in 1871, nearly twenty years before. Almost everyone in baseball believed that he was not only a great player but a great manager too.

There is a story about Cap and Cy that may or may not be true. One day, when Cy was still pitching for Canton, talk spread that Cap was in the grandstand watching the big pitcher. After the game, some local people asked him what he thought of Cy. Cap told the crowd he did not believe Cy was good enough to play for Chicago in the National League. The Canton folks were angry to hear that and probably told Cy. Now on August 6, he had his chance to show Cap how wrong he was.

Cy waited for the first Chicago batter to step up to home plate. He gripped the ball, ready to prove he belonged in the National League. He threw his mighty fastball for a strike. The Cleveland catcher, Charles "Chief" Zimmer, caught the ball easily, much better than the other catchers Cy was used to. At that time, a catcher wore only a small, thin glove, which did not help much in keeping that hand from getting swollen and bruised. But even with Cy throwing as hard as he could, Chief caught every ball without a miss.

The Chicago players were surprised that they were unable to score any runs in the first inning. They had thought Cy would be an easy target and anticipated getting plenty of hits and driving him from the game. Cy kept pitching as well as ever, holding the Colts to just one run in the entire game. He struck out five batters and allowed only three hits. Cleveland won by a score of 8–1, giving Cy his first win as a National League pitcher.

After the game, Cap went to a popular Cleveland hotel to find Davis Hawley, the man who had signed Cy to a contract. Cap tried to talk Mr. Hawley into selling Cy to Chicago for $1,000, a large amount of money at the time. Cap said the big pitcher needed a couple of years of experience before he would be of any use to Cleveland. Mr. Hawley smiled and reminded Cap that he had failed to get even one hit off Cy in four times at bat and did not see any reason to sell his new pitcher.

Cy would later say beating the Chicago Colts was one of the most rewarding things he ever did.[2]

Three days later, the Cincinnati Reds arrived in Cleveland for a game against the Spiders. Because of Cy's great game against Chicago a few days before, a large crowd of rooters filled the grandstand. At that time if you were a fan of the home team the newspapers called you either a rooter or a **crank.**

Cy pitched another good game, looking like a real veteran. The game was tied at 3–3 going into the tenth inning. Cincinnati scored a run in the **top half** of the inning to lead 4–3. The cranks worried that the game might be over, but the Spiders scored two runs in the **bottom half** of the inning to win 5–4. The Cleveland rooters cheered loudly and happily threw seat cushions onto the field. In the 1890s, baseball cranks, to show their excitement, threw seat cushions, **scorecards,** and even their straw hats right onto the field. Some of the rooters told the sportswriters it was the best game they had ever seen.

Cy had now won two games in a row. A Cleveland newspaper wrote, "Again Young Wins, The Cyclone Pitcher Does Better Work than Rhines."[3] (Billy Rhines was the Cincinnati pitcher.) The newspaper reported the crowd at the game was the biggest since July 4 and the largest crowd of the season for a Saturday. In just a few days, Cy had made a name for himself all around Cleveland.

On August 13, Cy won his third game, defeating Pittsburgh by a wild score of 20–9. He gave up three runs in the first inning and no more until the eighth. By then, Cleveland had a big lead, and Cy, probably a little tired, slowed down his pitches. With each game, he became more popular at home and in the other cities of the National League. Though opponents still called Cy "Rube" or "Farmer," he ignored them and continued to pitch well and win games.

The Cleveland Spiders were still not among the best teams in the National League. The only team with a worse record was Pittsburgh. The Spiders did not hit well and made many errors in the field. Because of this, Cy lost a few games even though he pitched well enough that he should have won. At the end of September, he had seven wins and seven losses, the only Cleveland pitcher without a losing record.

On October 4, the Spiders had two games to play with Philadelphia. It was the last day of the season and Cy asked for permission to pitch both games. He was not the first pitcher to try this, but still it was a hard thing to do. With the Cleveland rooters cheering him on, Cy won both games by scores of 5–1 and 7–3. The second game was stopped after seven innings because it was starting to get dark outside. There were no lights at ballfields at that time, and the late afternoon sun had begun to fade. The Spiders got credit for two wins, and Cy had shown enough strength to pitch sixteen innings in just one afternoon! His record for the 1890 season was nine wins and seven losses (or a **win-loss record** of 9–7), good for a pitcher in his first season.

When the final standings were printed, the Cleveland Spiders were still in second-to-last place. The team had only two good hitters, Ed McKean, who played **shortstop,** and George Davis, one of the outfielders. Cy was by far the best pitcher on the club. For the Spiders to improve in 1891, they would need to add some new players.

Mr. Robison, the owner of the Spiders, had several **streetcar** lines that ran from the east side of Cleveland all the way to the west side and back again. The streetcar cost five cents a ride, and the thousands of people who rode the cars had made Mr. Robison a rich man. He had the money to buy a few new players to help the team. In 1891, with Cy and several new teammates, the Spiders would be a much better team.

With the season over, Cy left Cleveland for his Gilmore home, where he immediately set to work. He woke up early in the morning to feed the animals, then went out to the faraway line of trees to chop wood. He was probably tired from the long baseball season, yet he continued to work from sunup to sundown. In late October, though, he became sick and had a high temperature. The town doctor came to visit and could see that Cy had typhoid fever.

In the last part of the nineteenth century, there was not much help for people who had a serious illness. One of the hardest to cure was typhoid fever, which often spread through water. Water from a stream or river or even a well might be dirty and filled with germs, and anyone who drank the unhealthy water had a strong chance of becoming sick. Cy's illness started with a high fever and likely a bad headache, coughing, and a painful stomachache. He became too tired to walk and had to lie in bed for most of the day. Without any useful medicine, the patient would take a long time to get well, sometimes two or three months.

Cy, being a young man, had a lot of strength that helped him fight the illness. His mother watched over him day and night until his fever went down and the headaches and coughing slowly stopped. That winter of 1890–91 was a tough one for Cy. Before his illness, he had liked to run several miles each day and then go hunting, a routine that he believed kept him ready to play ball. Because of the typhoid fever, he did not run or hunt or split wood or work the fields. When March came, Cy had to make plans to leave for spring training. He still needed time to get stronger but had no choice other than to pack his suitcase and leave for the Spiders training camp in Jacksonville, Florida.

DID YOU KNOW?

In 1882, there were two major leagues, the National League and the American Association. The National League began play in 1876, while the American Association's first season was 1882. After ten years, the Association broke apart, leaving the Nationals as the only major league.

THREE

LEAGUE PARK OPENS

Cleveland has now one of the finest ball parks in the country.

—*Cleveland Leader,* May 1891

THE TRAIN RIDE to Jacksonville, Florida, took several days. Most of the National League teams went south for the March sunshine and warm weather there. Players often gained weight in the winter, and they exercised in the hot sun to sweat off five or ten pounds. In the mornings, the Spiders would meet in their hotel lobby, then run a mile or two to the baseball park. They practiced hitting and fielding while the pitchers worked in the outfield, throwing balls to their catchers.

Near lunchtime, the players would run around the park a few times, then walk back to the hotel to eat and take some time to rest. In the afternoon, they had practice games, usually the experienced players against the new guys trying to win a place on the team. At the end of the day, they would either run or walk back to the hotel. The players did not have water bottles or energy drinks or even air-conditioning in

Portrait of Cy Young in his Cleveland Spiders uniform, about 1893.
Courtesy of National Baseball Hall of Fame and Museum, Cooperstown, NY

their hotel rooms. Those things came much later. Instead, the players sat in the lobby where there might be a breeze to keep them cool. Tomorrow would be another day of hard practice.

After a few weeks, Cy felt more like himself, able to throw and run as well as his teammates. He now had a contract that paid him $1,400 for the 1891 season. Today that amount would equal $38,000. If Cy were pitching now, even in his first season, his minimum baseball salary would be at least $555,000—a huge difference! Mr. Robison believed that Cy had the makings of a great pitcher and had given him a large increase in pay. Rather than buying fancy suits or diamond rings, Cy saved his money. In the next few years, he intended to buy his own farm in Gilmore. With a place to live, Cy would ask his neighbor Robba Miller to marry him. She was four years younger than Cy, but they had known each other for many years and wanted to be together for the rest of their lives. Robba, whom Cy called "Bobby," was a smart girl who knew something about baseball and already was Cy's biggest rooter.

In April, spring training came to an end. The Spiders had a good laugh when Cy happened to hear a marching band and followed it for several blocks through town. Most of the Cleveland players had seen many large parades, but Cy, being from the country, had not. Although he had lived in Cleveland and visited other big cities, the country boy in him won out and he ran to see the marchers.

Before the season opened, the Spiders added some new players to improve the team. Jimmy McAleer, a fast runner and outfielder, was put in at center field. Clarence "Cupid" Childs, a good hitter and second baseman, joined the **starting lineup,** while Oliver "Patsy" Tebeau was brought in to play third base. Mr. Robison expected his team to move up in the National League standings.

On April 22, the Cleveland Spiders started the season with four games in Cincinnati. Cleveland had to play eight games on the road before coming home. In his first National League season opener, Cy won his game 6–3. Spiders manager Bob Leadley picked Cy to let the rooters know who his number-one pitcher was.

After winning five of their first eight games, the Spiders came to Cleveland for the home opener. This day was extra special because Cy would pitch, and he would do it in a beautiful new stadium named League Park. When Frank Robison bought the Cleveland team, he had an idea to build a fine new ballpark that could hold 9,000 rooters. He found land on the east side of Cleveland at 66th Street and Lexington Avenue. Mr. Robison's streetcar line stopped at the new park, dropping off passengers only twenty feet from the ticket office. When the games were finished, most of the crowd climbed onto the streetcar for the ride back home. Some people would have driven their horse and buggy to the game, but Mr. Robison, a shrewd businessman, left no room for anybody to park carriages or horses, almost forcing them to ride the cars.

To make sure people visiting League Park had a fine afternoon, Mr. Robison built bathrooms for men and women. There were 120 **luxury boxes** for people who had extra money and wanted to sit in comfortable seats. Thirsty rooters could buy fresh lemonade, and there were

League Park, Cleveland, about 1910.
Author's Collection

sandwiches and popcorn for hungry fans. The Cleveland players had their own clubhouse with showers and a private entrance. There was no clubhouse for the visiting teams, who had to dress at their hotel.

Opening day at League Park took place on May 1. Two hours before game time, at least a thousand people stood in line at the two **ticket windows.** The lines were more than twenty-five feet long and getting longer by the minute. The Cleveland and Cincinnati players arrived on Mr. Robison's streetcars, each draped with red, white, and blue colors to celebrate opening day and the national flag. A large **brass band** played popular songs for the players and the crowd, as rooters gathered outside the park.

Since so many people were lined up at the ticket windows, the start of the game had to be moved from 3:00 to 4:00. Soon Mr. Robison realized he would have about 9,000 rooters for the game, the largest ever in Cleveland baseball history. When all the seats and long rows of wooden benches called bleachers were taken, ropes were put up in front of the outfield walls and a few hundred cranks stood there for the entire game.

At 4:08 p.m., Cy walked to the pitcher's box dressed in his brand-new Cleveland uniform. The shirt and pants were white, and black letters across his chest read "Cleveland." Cy had black socks that came up to his knees. His baseball shoes were black and reached above his ankles. This time the uniform fit perfectly, just the right size for a tall man like Cy.

Cy struck out the first Cincinnati batter while the crowd made more noise than the pitcher had ever heard on a baseball field. He did not allow a run until the eighth inning, when the Spiders already had a big lead. The final score was Cleveland 12, Cincinnati 3. While batting, Cy had gotten a single and scored a run. Though Cy could throw a ball faster than most pitchers, he did not run with much speed. The newspapers thought if Cy had been a faster runner, he might have been able to reach home more often.[1] It was all in fun, as the huge crowd cheered for Cy throughout the afternoon.

League Park exterior view, about 1910.
Author's Collection

Cy usually lived either in a downtown Cleveland hotel or at a boardinghouse near the ballpark. Most of the players stayed in boardinghouses that had private rooms and offered a home-cooked breakfast and sometimes dinner. Ballplayers making $100 to $300 a month could afford the weekly rent. In a good boardinghouse, a player could get a clean bed, a fireplace, and a jug of water and a bowl for washing up. Down the hallway was a bathroom that all the renters shared.

When Cy needed some new clothes or wanted to eat at a restaurant, he took the streetcar downtown. In 1891 Cleveland had 261,000 residents, making it the tenth-largest city in the country. Cleveland had a lot to offer, with fine restaurants, theaters, clothing stores, a modern ballpark, and a pretty good baseball team.

Near the end of the season, Chicago came to League Park with a chance to win the **pennant.** Cy always enjoyed pitching against Cap Anson and beating the team that had called him "Rube" and "Farmer." He did it again, winning 12–5 and ruining Chicago's hopes of finishing in first place. Cy had a terrific season for the Spiders, winning twenty-seven games, fifth best in the National League. He pitched 423 innings for seventh best in the league. Cy allowed fewer than three runs per game with an **earned run average (ERA)** of 2.85. The Spiders finished in fifth place, moving up two spots because of Cy's great pitching.

Cy returned once again to Gilmore at the end of the season to chop wood and spend time with Robba Miller, his soon-to-be wife. He was still thinking about buying some good land near Gilmore where he could start his own farm. In addition to that, he made plans to buy extra land, clear the fields for houses to be built, and then sell the land for a profit. Some years later, an article in *Sporting Life* magazine estimated that Cy had earned $10,000 buying and selling land. Only a person with good sense and clear thinking could have done this. Cy's talent for thinking ahead would make his life a lot easier. For now, though, he was saving his money.

Cy was now earning close to $2,000 a year, or $300 a month for the baseball season. A few of the Spiders earned that much, but most others received around $1,500. In the early 1890s, all the Spiders were getting a good salary, far above what people who worked in shops and factories could make. Some of the players on other teams earned as much as $3,000 for playing ball, but when the 1892 season began, many teams stopped paying the high salaries and forced their men to play for less. The players had no choice but to take a smaller salary or find another job outside baseball. At the time, the National League owners could do what they wanted because they were the only major league, and the players had to go along.

Because of the good weather and healthy water in Hot Springs, Arkansas, the Spiders went there to do their spring training for the 1892 season. One of the Cleveland newspapers asked Cy to write a letter about his experiences there, which it later published. Cy was not sure his letter was good enough for a newspaper to print. He said, "The thing of writing for the newspapers is a hard kind of business for me, but I will do the best I can."[2] Cy talked about the warm underground springs there. The hot water contained minerals, and many people believed that taking a bath in the mineral water or drinking it would cure their pains or illnesses. The downtown streets had the hot water piped to many of the street corners. People would bring a tin cup, fill it with water, and drink it slowly like a hot cup of coffee. Cy, too, believed the water had a healing effect on those who were sick.

On Sundays, Cy and a few of the Spiders walked to the Methodist church across from the hotel. After the service, he and his teammates went to a restaurant for lunch. The players had to use their own money to pay for their meals because the National League owners did not give them a daily allowance for food. That would not happen for several years.

At the end of spring training, the Spiders traveled to Memphis and Nashville, Tennessee, to play exhibition games. Mr. Robison's goal was to earn back the money he spent on the hotel rooms for the players while they trained. By the time the Spiders returned to Cleveland, Mr. Robison usually had covered his expenses for spring training.

On April 15, Cleveland opened the season at Cincinnati. The 1892 season would be much different, with the addition of four new clubs in the National League: Louisville, Kentucky; Washington, D.C.; Baltimore, Maryland; and St. Louis, Missouri. Now with twelve teams total, the league decided to divide the season in half. There would be a winner for the first half and one for the second half. In October, the two winners would play a series of games to determine the league champions.

Cy started the season by beating Cincinnati, 2–0. This was the first time in Cy's National League career that he held another team to no runs: a **shutout.** Springtime had not come to Cincinnati yet. Cy had to pitch in cold weather but stayed strong through the game.

Six days later, Cy pitched the opening day at Cleveland's League Park. For much of the afternoon, rain poured down on the field. At 4:00 the rain stopped, and the game began. Because of the bad weather, many rooters stayed home, yet 5,000 people attended and saw Cy win easily, 11–1.

To make things more convenient for the rooters, Mr. Robison built another ticket window, for a total of three. People who wanted the cheap twenty-five-cent tickets for seats far away from the field went to one window. Rooters who wanted to pay more money for a closer view went to the other two windows. Ladies had to pay for opening-day tickets, but they were allowed in free for all games during the week. Mr. Robison, like most gentlemen in the 1890s, believed that mothers and daughters should not have to pay to see his team play baseball. This helped bring more people to League Park and earn Mr. Robison extra money from his streetcars.

Throughout April and May 1892, Cy kept on winning. The year before, Cy had given up almost three runs a game. This year he made a big improvement by usually allowing fewer than two. In May, he pitched two more shutouts. It seemed whenever Cy was ready to pitch, the Spiders had a great chance to win.

On May 21, the Spiders were home at League Park to play St. Louis. Cy and his teammates played catch and ran around the field, waiting for the St. Louis club to arrive. At 4:00, the Cleveland players ran to their positions, but still there was no sign of St. Louis. The umpire waited a few minutes, then called a **forfeit** in favor of the Spiders. Cy got another win by just throwing one ball across home plate.

About forty-five minutes later, a bus loaded with the St. Louis players stopped at the park. They jumped off and ran quickly to the field. The team owner, in an attempt to save money, had counted on making the trip from St. Louis to Cleveland in fourteen hours instead of coming the day before and staying an extra night at a hotel. Because the players could not get to the field on time, a forfeit had already been called. In today's world, forfeits are unlikely since the players typically travel by airplane.

By June 16, the Cleveland weather had really heated up. There were 3,300 rooters in the stands watching Cy beat Louisville 10–2. Early in the game, many of the gentlemen in the crowd had taken off their dark suit jackets and rolled up their shirtsleeves. Even in hot weather, men always wore a suit, a tie, and a hat. The ladies wore long skirts that reached their shoes and blouses that buttoned up to their neck. They could not do anything about the heat other than bring an umbrella to keep the sun out of their eyes.

The hot weather did not hurt the Spiders. They were too far back in the standings to win the first half of the season but were still playing good baseball. On Monday, July 4, Independence Day, most people had a holiday from their jobs. All the National League teams played two games that day, one in the morning and one in the afternoon. Rooters could buy a ticket for either one game or both and watch baseball all day. For the two games, the Spiders had about 10,000 people at League Park. The rooters honored the holiday by lighting firecrackers and shooting guns into the air.

There were many great players in the National League, and Cy Young was one of them. He had gained a lot of respect by being a good friend to his teammates and by being kind to rooters and sportswriters. When the Cleveland team traveled to other cities, the newspapers wanted to talk to Cy and print what he said. In Chicago, for example, the sports reporter asked Cy about being called a "farmer" and a **"hayseed"** by some of the players. Cy said, "Oh yes, I am a farmer in the winter. There's no shame in being that. I am satisfied to let the boys call me 'Hayseed' as long as I come off the farm every spring in good health, something few players do when they winter in the city."[3]

Cy was able to stay calm when other teams called him names. He went out and pitched better than just about anyone, not caring what people called him. Soon, most of the players would call him "Cy" and nothing else.

On July 15, the first half, or spring season, ended with Boston as the winners. The Spiders still had a chance to win the second half and play Boston for the championship. With Cy pitching well and players like Cupid Childs, Jesse Burkett, and pitcher George Cuppy having good seasons, the Spiders were one of the best teams in the National League. They climbed to first place in early August and kept on winning.

In the second week of August, the Spiders led the National League with a record of 17–7. The Cleveland newspapers boosted the excitement by printing the starting lineups on the day of each game and giving the rooters more to read about and talk about before the games. Crowds at League Park got bigger every time the Spiders were at home.

On August 23, Cy won another home game against Philadelphia in eleven innings. The crowd stood up and shouted all through the game. In the tenth inning, with two men out, Cy got on base with a walk. Childs singled, and Cy ran all the way to third. Suddenly, Childs raced toward second, drawing away the attention of the Philadelphia infielders. Cy took a chance and headed for home plate. Remember, he ran a lot more slowly than most players. He was thrown out at home and walked to the bench trying to catch his breath. Even though he was tired, Cy pitched another strong inning, and the Spiders got a run to win the exciting game.

A week later, the Spiders scored an amazing twenty runs to make it easy for Cy to win again. Cleveland scored eight runs in the eighth inning alone! Baltimore got only three hits in the game, losing 20–1. The National League standings had Cleveland in first place with a win-loss record of 28–10. Boston was in second place with a 21–16 record. The race for the second-half pennant was on!

On Labor Day, September 5, the Spiders played in Philadelphia, one game in the morning and one in the afternoon. With almost 12,000 people watching, Cy won the second game 6–0. Of all the pitchers in the league, Cy had the most games without allowing a run. Most of the cranks believed Cleveland would win the second half because of Cy's great pitching.

At the end of September, Cy hit his first home run in his major league career. Usually pitchers were poor hitters, but on this day Cy surprised both teams by hitting the baseball far enough to easily run around the bases—even at his slow pace. The Spiders hit two more home runs to make it easy for Cy to win another game. Cleveland's record was now 47–17. They were just a few days away from winning the second-half championship.

On October 5, Cy pitched another shutout. He ended the regular season with thirty-six wins and twelve losses, the best in the National League. Cy pitched nine games in which he did not allow a single run, making him top in the National League once again. If that was not enough, he allowed the fewest runs per game! In 1892, nobody had pitched better than Cy Young, and now he would try to prove that to the world, playing Boston for the National League championship.

DID YOU KNOW?

The total number of people watching National League games on July 4, 1892, was 66,687! Playing baseball on our Independence Day holiday had become an American tradition that still is popular today.

THE FIRST TRY AT A CHAMPIONSHIP

The wood [hitting] was poor and Cleveland lost
the game.

—Cleveland Leader, 1892

O N OCTOBER 17, 1892, the first game of the championship series began. The team owners had decided to play nine games, and the first team to win five of them would be the champion. The first three games were to take place in Cleveland and the next three in Boston. If more games were needed to break a tie, the teams would move to New York, a neutral site, to finish the series.

The National League president, Nick Young, came to Cleveland to watch the games. He brought with him the owners of the ten other clubs that were not playing. They all agreed to have two umpires for the games, one behind home plate and one standing by first base. The home plate umpire called the balls and strikes, while the other umpire called the plays on the bases.

Cy started the game for the Spiders, while Jack Stivetts pitched for Boston. Both teams had trouble scoring runs against two of the best pitchers in the league. After nine innings, the score was 0–0. By the end of the eleventh inning, the sky had become dark. The umpires had no choice but to stop the game, calling it a tie.

Cy had pitched one of his best games, but so had Jack Stivetts. Now the Spiders could win only two games at home before leaving for Boston and possibly New York. The next day, John Clarkson pitched for the Spiders but lost to Boston 4–3. With just one day to rest, Cy agreed to pitch the third game. Although he did his best, the Spiders lost 3–2.

They were now behind Boston, two games to none. Cleveland had to win five of the next seven games to win the series, while Boston had to win only three. The two teams left Cleveland, taking the Lake Shore Railroad along with the umpires, President Nick Young, and the team owners. Some of the Spiders' rooters came along, paying extra money to see the games in Boston. The railroad had two special cars for the players, so they could stay away from the regular passengers and rest until they got to Boston.

The trip to Boston proved to be an unhappy one for Cy and his teammates. They lost all three games there, giving Boston the World Championship, five games to none. Cy had pitched twenty good innings at League Park but was unable to win a game in Boston.

Cy returned to Cleveland, packed his suitcase, and left for Gilmore. He had big plans to marry his sweetheart, Robba Miller. Cy had put away enough money and was sure he could take on the responsibility of starting a family life of his own. They were married at the Millers' home on the morning of November 8. For the time being, the newlyweds would live at the Young family home. They had four months to spend together before the start of another spring training. Bobby would have to get used to Cy leaving every March or April and not coming back until October. From all that is known, Bobby was a

Cy and Bobby Young in a wedding photo, 1892.
Courtesy of the Newcomerstown Historical Society, Newcomerstown, Ohio

strong woman who understood that her husband had to be away much of the time.

In early winter 1893, the National League made an important rule change. Up until then, pitchers had thrown from the box outlined on the ground, in which they could move around before throwing the baseball to home plate. Starting with the new season, a steel plate twelve inches long replaced the pitcher's box. The plate stood on a small mound not more than fifteen inches high. Now pitchers had to stand on the mound, place one foot on the steel plate (often called the rubber), and leave it there until the pitch was delivered. Most pitchers did not mind the change because they would now deliver the baseball moving downhill, which gave their pitches more force. In addition, the distance between the pitcher's spot and home plate was changed to sixty feet, six inches instead of fifty-five feet.

This change was made because Cy and a few other pitchers threw the ball too fast for the hitters to get a good swing. Moving the pitchers back five and a half feet gave the batters a moment longer to see the pitch. The National League believed the change would bring more hitting to the game and more excitement for the rooters. If the rule change worked, attendance at the games might go up and earn the teams more money.

Along with the change in the distance between the pitcher and home plate, there was talk about the use of gloves on the playing field. Some players had begun using gloves to protect their hands when fielding hard-hit **ground balls**. When professional baseball began in the late 1860s, only the catcher wore a thin glove on his hand to keep his fingers from getting bruised or broken. The infielders and outfielders wore no protection. Thirty years later, pitchers were throwing the ball harder, and baseballs came off the bat quicker.

In today's game, all players wear large mitts with plenty of padding inside, which is a great help in preventing fingers and hands from getting broken. Around the time Cy joined the Cleveland team, only a few of the Spiders players had started to wear a glove. Gloves made sense to some of the sportswriters and rooters, but others thought if you were a big, strong man you should not have to wear a glove to play baseball.

In March 1893, Cy signed his contract to play again with the Spiders. Mr. Robison had not decided whether to send the team to Hot Springs, Arkansas, or to have them stay in Cleveland to practice in a gym. Going to Arkansas meant paying for train tickets and hotels. By keeping the Spiders in Cleveland, Mr. Robison believed he could save money. The players could practice indoors and work just as hard as they did in Arkansas, though they would not get the chance to practice outside.

At the end of March, Mr. Robison changed his mind and sent his team south to Atlanta, Georgia, to start playing practice games. From there, the Spiders went on to play in Charleston, South Carolina; Chattanooga, Tennessee; and Savannah, Georgia. Each city had many baseball rooters who wanted to see teams from the National League. At each stop, the Spiders made money for Mr. Robison and helped pay the expenses for traveling.

Cy was able to get a few days off before the season started. He took a train to Newcomerstown and then a horse and carriage to Gilmore to spend time with his wife and parents. While Cy was at home, a Cleveland newspaper reporter visited to talk with him. Cy welcomed the writer by thoughtfully answering his questions and even showing him how to throw a **curveball.** Cy asked the reporter to come inside, where he introduced him to his mom and dad. Mrs. Young proudly told the writer that Denton was a good, kind son, just like his brothers.

The newspaper printed the story and added that Cy was well liked in all the cities where he played. The article told the readers about Cy's being a gentleman, not a ballplayer who argued with umpires and fought with other players. *Baseball Magazine* had a long article about

Union Station, Newcomerstown, Ohio, in the early 1900s.
Courtesy of the Newcomerstown Historical Society, Newcomerstown, Ohio

Cy, telling readers about his fair play, his honesty, and his common sense. At the age of twenty-six, Cy continued to earn a good name for himself both at home and on the baseball field.

On April 27, the Spiders opened the regular season in Pittsburgh. There was a grand parade to the stadium with a marching band playing popular music to the rooters lined up along the city streets. A crowd of 8,000 happy people filled the grandstands, eager to see baseball once again. In the seats were several hundred **newsboys** and **bootblacks.** They were mostly poor boys who sold papers or shined shoes instead of going to school. On this day, the Pittsburgh newspaper treated the boys to free admission to a National League game.

With Cy pitching, the Spiders won the opener 7–2. In Cleveland, rooters gathered at the **telegraph** and newspaper offices to get the results of the game—they could not wait until the next morning to find out who had won.

A week later, the Cleveland team returned to League Park for the home opener. The weather was cold, and the rooters wore their winter coats during the game. Cy pitched well until the seventh inning, when Chicago scored two runs to break a 3–3 tie. The Spiders could not score any more runs and lost the game 5–3.

On July 4, Cleveland was home at League Park for the holiday **doubleheader.** A huge crowd of 17,000 rooters attended, the biggest total since 1889! Many of the men in the grandstands had brought pistols and firecrackers, firing them whenever the Spiders made a good play. In the second game, Ed McKean hit a long home run over the right-field wall. It was the first time a Cleveland player had ever hit a ball that cleared the high fence in front of Lexington Avenue.

Near the end of the month, the Spiders were in Cincinnati for a game against the Reds. The teams waited for the umpire to arrive, but for some reason he did not make it to the ballpark. Instead of canceling the game, the teams agreed to play with one member of each team calling the balls and strikes. It turned out to be a bad decision for Cleveland, which lost the game 4–3.

THE TELEGRAPH AND BASEBALL

To find out how the Spiders were doing when out of town, the newspapers had telegraph machines to give them the latest information. The machines had electric wires connecting them to wooden poles high above city streets. The wires connected telegraph offices around Cleveland to other large cities like Philadelphia, Boston, and New York. The telegraph operators used a code—called Morse code—to send messages through the wires linking the cities. A message sent from Philadelphia was received by the Cleveland operator, who then wrote down the code on a sheet of paper and figured out the message. That way, newspaper reporters could find out what had happened during the game and write a quick story about it.

Since the Spiders were playing so well in the 1892 season, all the reporters at the newspapers crowded around the telegraph operator, eager to find out the score. They all went away happy when Cleveland won its games. Soon the papers would have to build a bigger room for all the people trying to get into the telegraph office.

The Reds player who was umpiring called nine walks against Cy, allowing Cincinnati to get extra runners on base and score runs. Even on a bad day, Cy would not walk anywhere near nine players. The newspaper reporters believed the Reds player had been unfair and had pretended many of Cy's strikes were balls, giving Cincinnati a win they probably had not earned.

The 1893 season did not go well for the Spiders. Although Cy won a great thirty-four games, Cleveland ended with a record of 73–55 and finished in third place. In 1892, the Spiders had won ninety-three games and the second-half championship. This time, they could not catch Boston, and the Cleveland players left for home, upset they had not played better.

When the season ended, Cy returned to Gilmore for a short time. In October, he and Bobby left for Chicago to see the 1893 World's Fair. Over 27 million people from all parts of the world visited Chicago that year to see the newest inventions, art, beautiful diamonds, and jewelry and to take a ride on the very first Ferris Wheel.

President Grover Cleveland started the fair by giving a speech and touring some of the buildings and exhibits. Large crowds followed the president as he walked through the pavilions and spoke with many people from around the world. Each state in the Union had its own building to display the best things it had to offer. There were over two hundred buildings to visit that had artwork, inventions, and all types of music from big bands to singers and piano players. No doubt Mr. and Mrs. Young had a wonderful time.

During the long winter months, Cy and Bobby had a lot of time to spend together. They enjoyed quiet evenings, reading or just talking until it was time for bed. They visited friends around the county and wrote letters to brothers and sisters who had moved away.

Cy and Bobby liked to have fun, as Cy would tell in stories later in his life. One of those was about Bobby, who one day went hunting with her husband. They had a good day, bringing home several rabbits. Cy asked a friend who owned a camera to come to the house. He had Bobby hold one of the rabbits right in front of the camera lens and stand back as far as she could. When the picture was taken and developed, the rabbit looked as tall as Bobby! When out-of-town reporters came to see Cy, he would tell them about the five-foot rabbits in Tuscawaras County and show them the picture to prove it.

In early 1894, Cy received his contract from Mr. Robison. For the first time in his baseball career, he was unhappy with the money offered. The National League owners had decided that no player could earn more than $2,400. It is not known what Cy was offered, but he let Mr. Robison know he did not like the contract and would not sign it unless the pay was increased.

Cy was not the only Cleveland player unhappy about his contract. Teammates Jesse Burkett, Ed McKean, and Chief Zimmer were just as

THE RESERVE CLAUSE

The National League had a rule named the Reserve Clause. It meant an owner of a ball club had the right to keep a player as long as he wanted. The owner could send the player a contract each year, and the player had no choice but to accept it or not play baseball at all. The only thing a player could do was try to talk with his team owner and get a better salary.

In 1969, Curt Flood, a player for the St. Louis Cardinals, filed a lawsuit against Major League Baseball to end the Reserve Clause. The suit went to the Supreme Court, where the judges voted 5–3 in favor of the Major Leagues and the team owners. In 1975, the players' union negotiated to end the Reserve Clause and were allowed to become **free agents** after six years of service.

angry with Mr. Robison. These players were stars of the league and believed, as Cy did, that they should get more money to play.

In mid-March, the Spiders reported to Cleveland for spring training, but Cy stayed in Gilmore. He waited until March 26 before meeting with Mr. Robison and signing his contract. It is not known if he got the raise he wanted, but Cy would remember the problem for quite a long time.

DID YOU KNOW?

At Cleveland's League Park, any ball hit over the outfield wall could be picked up and returned to the ticket office for a free seat in the grandstand. Children waited outside the park, and when a ball came flying over the wall, the race began. The winner ran to the office, returned the ball, and got a ticket to see the rest of the game.

FIVE

THE TEMPLE CUP

Young will pitch tomorrow and we think the trophy
will come our way, of course.

—Patsy Tebeau (Cy Young files,
National Baseball Hall of Fame and Museum)

T HE 1894 SEASON was another disappointment for Cy, the Spiders, and Mr. Robison. Cy won twenty-six games, but he lost twenty-one, the most in his career since 1891. The Spiders won only sixty-eight games and finished in sixth place. Since 1890, Cy's first year with Cleveland, the team had improved almost every season. They had played for the championship in 1892, and had finished third in 1893. The rooters deserted League Park, which made Mr. Robison angry at his players and just about everyone else.

As spring arrived in 1895, the rooters didn't know what to expect for the new season. Would the Spiders bounce back and have a good year? Or another bad one? Soon they would find out because it was time for the players to leave for Arkansas and spend a few weeks training at Hot Springs. Cy signed his 1895 contract early but asked for one thing to be added. Cy did not want to pitch any games on Sundays. Mr. Robison and manager Tebeau agreed and made sure that Cy would pitch either a Saturday or Monday game.

In the 1890s and into the twentieth century, many people believed that Sunday was a day of rest and that activities like baseball games should not take place. Some cities in the United States, like Cleveland, had laws that said Sunday baseball could not be played within the city limits. Cy knew that a Sunday game was unlikely, but if it did happen, he wanted to be able stay on the bench.

At the end of spring training, Cy became sick and had to take a break from pitching. In early April, the newspapers reported he had either **malaria** or **tonsillitis** or possibly the grippe (flu). Cy could not pitch the April 18 opener against Cincinnati. He rested another nine days, then started his first game against Louisville. He pitched well enough, winning the game by a score of 4–3. As the season went on, Cy got stronger and pitched his first shutout of the year on June 14 against the New York Giants. The Spiders scored only one run, but that was all they needed for the 1–0 win. Cy allowed only five hits and struck out seven batters.

With Cy doing well, the Spiders moved into third place, behind Boston and Pittsburgh. Once again, the Cleveland rooters began to get excited about their team. Near the end of June, a giant baseball was put up in front of the Cuyahoga Building in downtown Cleveland, the offices of Mr. Robison. The baseball could be seen from several blocks away. If the day was rainy, people could look out their windows to see if the ball was still there. If it was taken inside, that meant the game was canceled because of the weather. Now the rooters did not have to take the streetcar all the way to League Park just to find out whether the game would be on.

On July 4, the Spiders were in Pittsburgh for the holiday double-header. Since both teams were in the running for first place, the crowd at the games broke the attendance record at Exposition Park. The total was 30,000 rooters, 14,000 for the first game and 16,000 for the second.

There were at least 2,000 to 3,000 people there from Cleveland. Baseball was getting more and more popular each year. Because the crowd was too large for everyone to get a seat, ropes were set up on the field in front of the left-field and center-field grandstands for the extra rooters to stand behind. The umpires ruled any ball hit beyond the ropes would be a triple.

In the first game, with Cy pitching, the Spiders trailed 3–1 in the eighth inning. One of the Pittsburgh batters hit a **line drive** right at Cy. It came so fast he could not get out of the way, and the force of the hit knocked him down. Manager Tebeau wanted Cy to leave the game and go back to the hotel to rest. Cy refused and kept on pitching even though he was hurt. Pittsburgh scored three more runs, and the game was lost. Cy probably should have let someone else finish the game, but he was a great competitor and did not want to let his teammates down.

Two weeks later and feeling much better, Cy pitched one of the season's best games. He beat the first-place Baltimore Orioles, 1–0. Cy allowed just four hits, and he batted in the game's only run. One of the Cleveland newspapers wrote about the ball game, "It was a game that should go down in baseball history that the rooter of today (1895) should take his grandchildren on his knee and tell of the time Cleveland gave the champion Baltimores their first shut out of the season."[1]

On July 20, Cy beat Brooklyn by the score of 2–1. The other National League cities were starting to notice how well the Spiders were playing and just how great a pitcher they had in Cy Young. The *New York Mercury* newspaper wrote about Cy not just as a ballplayer but as a good man: "There is a pitcher who works hard, takes care of himself and does not indulge in sprees nor brawls. Here's to you Cy!"[2] Some of the Spiders and many other players around the National League liked to argue with the umpires and fight with each other, but Cy was not one of them.

Cy was having his best season ever, and the Spiders were playing very well. They were right behind Baltimore in the battle for first place. On July 22, Cy beat Washington 8–6, and Cleveland landed in the top spot. For the rest of the year, the Spiders and Orioles fought each other for the pennant. Through August and September, the two teams stayed close together, sometimes less than a game apart. Cy continued to win game after game on his way to an incredible season.

On September 15, Cleveland was in St. Louis for a rare Sunday game. The city had no laws against playing Sunday baseball. The game was not going well for the Spiders when Cy told manager Tebeau he would pitch if needed, even though his contract said he did not have to play on Sundays. With the pennant still possible, he entered the game and helped the Spiders come from behind and win 8–5.

The season ended with Cleveland in second place, just behind Baltimore. The Spiders had put up a great fight but came up a little short. There was no time to be upset, because the first- and second-place teams were to play each other for the right to be called the champions of the National League. This was a change from 1892, when the season had been divided into two halves, and the first-half winner had played the second-half winner. Seven games were to be played, and the first team to win four games would receive the championship trophy called the Temple Cup. One of the owners of the Pittsburgh club, William Temple, had donated the cup to be given to the winning team. In addition, all the money from ticket sales went to the players, with the champs getting 60 percent and the losers 40 percent. Both teams were eager to play and earn extra money for themselves and their families.

The first three games were to be played at League Park, the next three in Baltimore, and a seventh game, if needed, at a different city agreed on by both teams. Of course, the Spiders wanted to win the first three games in Cleveland and go to Baltimore needing to win just one more. The league again decided to have two umpires at each game, one behind home plate and one in the infield, perhaps because the Baltimore players had a reputation for breaking the rules whenever they could. With two umpires watching, the chances were better the Orioles would behave themselves.[3]

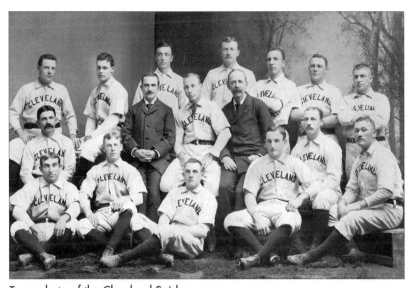

Team photo of the Cleveland Spiders.

Courtesy of National Baseball Hall of Fame and Museum, Cooperstown, NY

The games at League Park were scheduled for Wednesday, October 2, and Thursday, October 3, with a day off before game three on Saturday, October 5. On Sunday, both teams would ride a special train to Baltimore to play again on Monday. The Cleveland newspapers urged the local rooters to travel to the games and cheer for the Spiders.

It would take more than cheering to beat the Baltimore Orioles. They had great players like Willie Keeler, John McGraw, Hughie Jennings, and pitcher Bill Hoffer. They could hit better than most teams, **steal** bases, and make the tough plays in the outfield and infield. Another reason why Baltimore won so many games was that some of the players did not follow the rules of baseball. They would push and shove runners off the bases and tag them out. With only one umpire watching, it was easier to get away with cheating. Most other teams in the National League followed the rules, but the Orioles sometimes broke them and hardly ever got caught.[4] Now, with two umpires on the field, they had to be much more careful.

On Wednesday, the teams met at League Park for game number one. The temperature was sixty-five degrees, perfect for a fall afternoon. Mr. Robison kept the scoreboard blank, hoping to force the crowd of nearly 7,000 to buy scorecards instead. After all, the ticket money was going to the players, and Mr. Robison believed he should earn something.

Cy, who had won thirty-five games during the regular season, walked to the mound and stepped on the rubber. The hometown rooters cheered for him and blew horns while shaking cowbells and baby rattles. Cy pitched a great game, and the score was tied at 2–2 going into the ninth inning. The Orioles took the lead when John McGraw hit a double to score Wilbert Robinson from second base. The Spiders came to bat in the bottom of the ninth needing one run to tie the game and another to win. Jesse Burkett, the top hitter in the National League, drove a double into the outfield. Then Ed McKean hit a single, and Burkett raced home to tie the game at 3–3. Two more hits **loaded the bases,** with Chief Zimmer coming to bat and only one out. Cy's favorite catcher hit a ground ball, and the Orioles infielders tried to get a double play. The throw to first was a little late, and McKean crossed home plate, scoring the winning run. The Cleveland rooters ran out of the grandstands and onto the field to congratulate the Spiders.

The next day, all seats at League Park were sold out before game number two began. Now that the Spiders had won a game, the rooters were thrilled about their team's chances. One gentleman who called himself a local crank wrote a poem to the newspapers urging on the Spiders to win. The Cleveland papers liked to call the Orioles the "Oysters," probably because Baltimore was on the East Coast of the United States and seafood was popular there. The man who wrote the poem must have liked oysters too:

> *Come Patsy get your Spiders out,*
> *And rub them o'er and o'er.*

For Skipper Hanlon pulling hard,
To reach this tranquil shore.
He's got on board an Oyster load,
The first to be found,
So get your Spiders buttered up,
To fry those Oysters brown.[5]

"Patsy" in the poem referred to the Spiders' manager, Patsy Tebeau, and "Skipper Hanlon" was the manager of the Orioles.

By game time, ropes had been put behind the first- and third-base lines with rooters four rows deep. So that everyone could see the field, the first row sat down, the second row kneeled, the third row bent over, and the last row stood straight up. Along with the loud and happy crowd, a group of rooters brought a giant eight-foot horn with six tubes attached. They laid it against one of the grandstand railings while six people blew into the tubes at once. It must have made quite a noise, but nobody, except a few Baltimore cranks, had any problem with it.

Before the teams took the field, a small group of rooters walked out of the stands and up to the Cleveland bench. For his big win the day before, they gave Cy a brand-new shotgun and several packages of shells. Happy with the gift, Cy walked to home plate, loaded the gun, and fired it into the air. With that, game two of the Temple Cup series began.

George Cuppy pitched the game for the Spiders. George, Cleveland's number-two pitcher, had won twenty-six games during the regular season and won again that day, 7–2. Jesse Burkett had four hits to lead the Spiders to their second straight victory. Several Cleveland rooters had misbehaved, throwing a pop bottle onto the field and setting off firecrackers. The Baltimore reporters saw this, and in the next day's papers, people in the Orioles' hometown read stories about how the terrible Cleveland rooters had thrown stones, potatoes, eggs, and bottles at the Baltimore players. This was not true, but the Baltimore cranks believed it and made plans to get revenge when the Spiders came to Baltimore.

The Cleveland papers denied the exaggerated stories. They admitted that one pop bottle and a single potato had been thrown, but that was all. Mr. Robison offered a $25 reward to anyone who gave him the names of the men throwing things on the field. He told the papers there would not be any pop sold for Saturday's game to make sure no bottles could be thrown at the players.

On Saturday afternoon, the teams met for game three, the last to be played in Cleveland. Even though he had only two days of rest, Cy was chosen as the starting pitcher for Cleveland. Manager Tebeau wanted to go to Baltimore with a three-game lead. Having Cy pitch again gave the Spiders their best chance to win.

Once more, the game was sold out, with between 15,000 and 17,000 rooters squeezed into League Park. Again ropes were strung down the third- and first-base lines. Extra ropes were put in the outfield between left and center field. The newspapers reported sixty-five men had climbed bravely to the roof of the park, sitting with their legs dangling over the side. Other rooters who could not get a ticket climbed trees and telegraph poles outside the park for a view of the game. More people stood on the rooftops of homes and buildings to get even a faraway view. It was the biggest crowd to see a ball game at League Park since it had opened in 1891.

Cy was not affected by the gigantic crowd, and he pitched another wonderful game. The Spiders scored three runs in the first inning, and that was all Cy needed. The Orioles were able to score only one run, and that was in the eighth inning. In eighteen innings of work, Cy gave up a total of four runs, or only two per game. With pitching like that, even the mighty Orioles had little chance to win. The final score read Cleveland 7, Baltimore 1. Now the Spiders had to win only one of the next four games to claim the Temple Cup.

On Sunday, the teams left Cleveland for the train ride to Baltimore. The Cleveland players knew that the Orioles would be ready for game four, but they did not know how angry the Baltimore rooters would be. On Monday morning, the Spiders climbed into a horse-drawn wagon to take them to the Orioles' ballpark. Along the route to the ballpark, crowds of people waited with rotten apples and eggs. The players dropped down on the wagon floor to avoid being hit. The attack kept up all the way to the park, where the Spiders had to jump out of the wagon and run to the visitor's gate.

When the game began, people in the grandstand threw bricks and potatoes at the Cleveland players. Some of the bricks landed near the Spiders in the infield, just a few feet away from third baseman James "Chippy" McGarr. Some of the Baltimore players yelled to the crowd to stop throwing things and leave the players alone. The rest of the game was more peaceful, but it must have made the Cleveland players nervous. The Spiders failed to score any runs and were easily beaten, 5–0. When the game ended, about 1,500 Orioles rooters charged after the Spiders. The players ran as fast as they could and hid under the grandstands.

Several minutes later, the Baltimore police led the Spiders out through the Orioles' clubhouse in hope that the cranks would not notice. It worked for a couple of minutes, but the rooters saw the wagon and ran up to the horses. Several people tried to take the harnesses off the horses, so the wagon could not move away. The police pushed back the rooters, and the wagon moved slowly forward. People began again to throw bricks and dirt at the Spiders, who again lay on the floor of the wagon to protect themselves. Police stood on the driver's seat and on the steps of the wagon to try to stop the brick throwing. Although they did their best, several bricks reached the Spiders, one hitting Cupid Childs squarely on the head. The next day he had a bump the size of a large walnut. The Spiders finally made it back to the hotel, where several of the players carried bricks to take home as souvenirs.

The next day, the Spiders returned to the ballpark for game five. A large group of policemen did everything they could to get the players onto the field safely. Cy was chosen to pitch and try to end the series right there. Once again, the Baltimore hitters were helpless against Cy's fastballs and curves. At the end of six innings, neither team had been able to score a single run. Then in the seventh, the Baltimore rooters moaned as they watched the Spiders score three runs. The Orioles were able to answer with one run in the bottom half. An inning later, Cleveland added two more runs to give Cy a 5–1 lead. In the bottom of the ninth, Cy allowed his second run while walking two batters and hitting another to load the bases. With the crowd screaming and two outs, Cy got the last batter to hit an easy ground ball for the final out. The Spiders won 5–2 and were National League champions! Of the four victories, Cy won three, including the last one needed to beat Baltimore for the championship.

When the Spiders were ready to leave the ballpark, a team of seventy-five policemen waited to ride with the players back to the hotel. With their help, everybody had a safe trip, without any bricks or rocks being thrown. Now the only problem was how to get to the train station for the trip home without the local rooters seeing them. Manager Tebeau had a smart idea. He decided to have the players leave two at a time every few minutes. By having everyone leave this way, the team did not attract any attention from Baltimore cranks ready to throw more apples and bricks.

On the way back to Cleveland, the train stopped in Alliance, Ohio, to take on more passengers. Several hundred Cleveland rooters were waiting on the platform to cheer the Spiders. Out came Cy to wave to the crowd and say a few words of thanks. From Alliance, the train continued to Cleveland, where hundreds more people gathered to greet the champions.

The players stepped down from the train to a salute of firecrackers. A gentleman gave manager Tebeau a large box of cigars to hand out to the players. People waved flags and cheered as the Spiders waved back and said thanks to the crowd. There was a party for the team the next day, and on October 24, Cy Young and Chief Zimmer were the guests of honor at the Army and Navy Hall. It had been a great year for the city of Cleveland and the Spiders, one that would be remembered for a long time.

DID YOU KNOW?

In the early days of the National League, when there was
only one umpire per game, many base runners went from
second base to home plate without touching third. With
a man on second and the batter getting a base hit to the
outfield, the umpire ran to the **pitcher's mound** to watch the
batter rounding first base. The runner at second knew this
and would skip third base on purpose to get home faster.
This trick ended when a second umpire was added.

SIX

CY CHANGES TEAMS

Of all the pitchers in the country, no one did better
work than the veteran Cy Young.

—Hugh Duffy, 1902 (Cy Young files,
National Baseball Hall of Fame and Museum)

OVER THE WINTER of 1895 and into 1896, Cy kept to his usual routine, working on the farm and hunting, this time with the new shotgun his friends had given him during the Temple Cup series. On March 3, he arrived in Cleveland early to help his catcher Chief Zimmer in some indoor baseball games. A few days later, Cy and the Spiders left for Arkansas again to train for the new season.

The first days in Hot Springs were too cold for practice. Instead, the players took a long hike in the mountains and then returned to camp for hot baths. When the weather warmed, the Spiders began their early-morning routine of a one-mile run followed by practice until 11:30. After lunch, they practiced again before playing exhibition games.

The new season began on April 16 at St. Louis in front of 15,000 rooters. Cy gave up several runs in the late innings and lost the game,

Cy and Bobby at Hot Springs, Arkansas, about 1900.
Courtesy of Temperance Tavern Museum, Newcomerstown, Ohio

5–2. The Spiders played away from home for the first nine games, returning to Cleveland for the home opener on April 30.

Cy allowed one run in the first inning, and that was the only one
Cincinnati managed to score. The Spiders won the well-pitched game,
2–1. With the home opener behind them, the Spiders focused on the
race for the pennant. They had a good season but fell far behind the
Baltimore Orioles, who once again finished in first place. Cleveland
won eighty games, which left them in second place and set up a re-
match with the Orioles for the Temple Cup. This time, the first three
games were to be played in Baltimore, the next three in Cleveland, and
if needed, a seventh game in a city to be decided by the players. Cy, who

had won twenty-eight games in the regular season, was picked to start game one at Union Park, the home of the Orioles.

The Spiders left Cleveland for the long train ride east to Baltimore. They passed through Youngstown and Pittsburgh without any problems. A short time later, the train stopped on the tracks because of a terrible accident several miles ahead. The Cleveland players were told that several people had been killed in the crash and that others were badly hurt. Some of the cars had gone off the track, but most of the broken train still stood on the rails, making any travel east impossible.

The Baltimore and Ohio Railroad Company had to telegraph all the trains heading east toward Maryland to stop where they were until the tracks were cleared. Manager Tebeau tried to find another route for the team to travel, but nothing could be done. The players waited all night and into the morning, when the train finally moved forward until it reached the site of the wreck. The Spiders got off the train and walked to a new train that was brought in from the east, on the other side of the wreck. From there, they reached Baltimore on Thursday, seven hours late. They had to postpone the opening game until Friday.

On October 2, the first game of the Temple Cup series began. This time, the Baltimore rooters did not bring any bricks or stones to throw at the Spiders. Many of them were angry because the Orioles owner had raised the **general admission** price from twenty-five cents to fifty cents. Because of the higher price, attendance at the game was no more than 5,000.

In the bottom of the first inning, John McGraw led off for Baltimore. Cy threw his first pitch and McGraw hit a hard drive right back at the Spiders pitcher. He could not get his glove out in front of him fast enough, and the speeding ball hit him on the wrist. Cy was hurt, but he did not want his teammates to know. By the seventh inning, the score was 3–1 in favor of Baltimore. As the game neared the end, two of Cy's fingers started to swell, making it tough for him grip the ball. The Orioles saw some easy pitches to hit and scored three more runs. The first game was lost, 7–2. Whether it was the long train ride or perhaps Cy's injured wrist, the Spiders lost both remaining games and headed back to Cleveland down three games to none.

The teams were supposed to play again on Wednesday, October 7, but the weather was so cold—not quite fifty degrees—that the game was canceled. The next day, the temperature barely reached forty-eight degrees, yet both teams agreed to play in the bad weather. Cy could not pitch because of his sore wrist, and the Spiders lost game four, 5–0. That evening, the players met at the Hollenden House, where the Spiders brought out the Temple Cup and placed it on the bar of the hotel restaurant. The cup was filled with **champagne,** which everybody drank until it was empty. Then the Spiders congratulated the winners and gave them the cup to take home to Baltimore.

With two Temple Cup series behind them, it looked as though the Spiders would be fighting for another pennant when the 1897 season began. Much to the Cleveland rooters' surprise, their team finished in fifth place with a record of 69–62. Cy had the worst season of his career, with a record of 21 and 19. The newspapers believed Cy had pitched too many games over the last two years, which might have been true. In 1895 and 1896, Cy had pitched 98 games and 784 innings, a tremendous number.

Even though the season did not go well, there were two great events for Cy. In spring training, the Spiders brought in a young catcher named Lou Criger. The new man, born in Elkhart, Indiana, was twenty-five years old. Lou was not a big guy, standing 5 feet, 10 inches tall and weighing only 165 pounds. Chief Zimmer, the Spiders' regular catcher, weighed about 190 pounds. Though Criger did not have Zimmer's size, he could stand at home plate and take the pounding he got from runners trying to knock him over and force him to drop the ball. Lou had a strong arm, which helped him throw out runners trying to steal second or third base.

Lou spent the 1897 season as a part-time catcher, playing in only thirty-nine games. During that time, he became close friends with Cy, a friendship that lasted for the remainder of their lives. He would become Cy's permanent catcher for twelve years and more than four hundred games. It was Lou's job to decide what pitches Cy or any other pitcher should throw and to signal him with the fingers on his right hand. His hand would be just inside his right leg so only Cy could see it. A fast ball might be one finger and a curveball two. Cy later said he always agreed with whatever pitch Lou called for, never **shaking off** his signs in any ball game.[1]

The other great event for Cy happened on September 18. He beat Cincinnati 6–0 without allowing a single base hit! It was Cy's first no-hitter in the National League and one of the best games he ever pitched. He walked one batter, and the Spiders made a few errors, but none of the Cincinnati batters could hit safely against Cy's great pitching. The last no-hitter in the National League had taken place in 1893, four years before.

In the 1898 season, the Spiders and Cy played much better baseball. The Spiders won eighty-one games, and Cy had twenty-five victories. He allowed an average of fewer than three runs a game, his best total since 1892. Even though the team did well, Mr. Robison was unhappy with the small number of rooters attending games at League Park. He became annoyed enough to change the Cleveland home games to away games from the end of August to the end of September as a way to punish the Cleveland rooters by not allowing them to see any National League baseball.

In May 1898, the owner of the St. Louis team ran out of money, and the National League decided to sell the club after the season ended. Mr. Robison remembered opening day of 1896, when the Spiders played in St. Louis. The attendance at that game had been 15,000, a crowd that had impressed the Cleveland owner. He did not say anything to the newspapers but started to make plans to buy the St. Louis team. In 1898, no rules stopped any owner from having more than one club in the same league.

In late February 1899, the papers reported that Mr. Robison was interested in buying the St. Louis team. He claimed that the story was not true and that the Spiders would open the season in April as usual. A month later, the news broke that Mr. Robison indeed had bought the St. Louis team and was planning to transfer his best players there. That meant Cy, manager Patsy Tebeau, Jesse Burkett, Ed McKean, Cupid Childs, and others would be sent to St. Louis as members of the Perfectos, the new team nickname.

Though he did not want to leave Cleveland, Cy made the move to St. Louis and pitched the opener on April 15, 1899, against—of all teams—the Cleveland Spiders! The team had many new faces, most of them average to poor baseball players. The Spiders were now run by Stanley Robison, the brother of Frank Robison. Unlike his brother, Stanley did not have a good understanding of baseball, and his Cleveland team had a terrible season. On opening day, Cy had no trouble from the Spiders, winning 10–1 in front of 15,000 St. Louis rooters.

In his first year with the Perfectos, Cy won twenty-six games with only sixteen losses. Once again, he allowed fewer than three runs per game and led the league with forty complete games. In Cy's time, a pitcher was expected to start and finish each game and Cy did that forty times! On August 18, Cy pitched a shutout against the Philadelphia Phillies, winning 8–0. Three days later, he did it again, beating Chicago by the score of 2–0. This was great pitching, but Cy was not finished. On August 24, he faced Philadelphia again, a team that had some of the greatest hitters in the game: Ed Delahanty, Nap Lajoie, and Elmer Flick. Even against these excellent batters, Cy threw his third straight shutout and won 5–0. In twenty-seven innings of pitching, he had not given up a single run! Even with this great accomplishment, Cy remained modest as ever. He told the newspapers, "I am not so much to blame for it all as the other fellows (Philadelphia) they were not batting at their usual gait."[2] Instead of patting himself on the back, he tried to say the Phillies batters were not their usual selves.

St. Louis had a fine season, winning eighty-four games while losing sixty-seven. It seemed Mr. Robison had made a smart choice with his purchase of the team, leaving brother Stanley to handle the Spiders in Cleveland. Earlier in the year, Frank Robison had said he would do his best to make sure Cleveland had a good team. He did not keep his word. The Spiders became the worst club in the league, finishing in last place. The National League owners became angry at the poor showing of the Spiders team and dropped them from the league. Going into the 1900 season, there was no National League baseball in Cleveland.

Mr. Robison had made enemies in his old town, but he thought everything in St. Louis would turn out well. He had no idea the 1900 season would be a big failure. For the first time in his career, Cy had an injury that forced him to stay on the bench for several weeks. He only won nineteen games while losing the same number. He still allowed just three runs a game and threw four shutouts, but the Perfectos fell apart, winning only sixty-five games and losing seventy-five.

In the middle of October, Mr. Robison sent out a terrible letter to his players. He first said most of the team would not receive their final paychecks until later. He mentioned four players who were not affected by this declaration, but Cy was not one of them. Mr. Robison believed his team had not tried hard enough to win and had spent too much time in **saloons** and at the racetrack betting on horses. Mr. Robison warned the players they might have their salaries cut because of their bad play during the season.

Cy must have been hurt by the letter, being included as one of the men not giving their best for the team. He said nothing to the papers in October, but simply packed his suitcases and returned to Gilmore. Some of the other players spoke out and claimed they had done nothing wrong, but Cy refused to join with them. Cy had played for Mr. Robison his entire time in the National League. The letter was an awful thing and probably should not have been sent. Cy always gave his best effort, and most people in baseball knew that.

While Cy chopped wood and went hunting, a group of men got together and planned to start a new baseball league. They would call it the American League, and it was to have no connection with the National League. The new league would form its own teams, pick the cities to play in, build new ballparks, and find players to fill the rosters. Unlike the National League, the new league would not have any limit on salaries. Since the new league had nothing to do with the old one, the organizers saw no reason not to write letters to players like Cy and ask them to join. With the letters were promises of a lot more money.

For the first time in his career, Cy had the chance to choose where he wanted to play. The National League owners could keep players on their teams as long as they wanted, but they had no way of stopping any player who wanted to leave to join the American League. For once, the players had the freedom to choose where they wanted to play, though even then, it was only for a year or two.

In early 1901, Cy received a letter from the Boston team of the American League. They offered him more pay if he would leave St. Louis and join their team, called the Boston Americans. It helped a lot when Cy learned that Lou Criger, his favorite catcher, was going to join the Boston team. Near the end of March, Cy let the baseball world know he would sign with Boston and try out the American League.

The news was a major loss for Mr. Robison. He had counted on Cy since 1890 and now had to find another great pitcher. Cy, in talking to the newspapers, mentioned Mr. Robison's letter from the previous October. "I worked ten years for Mr. Robison and never **shirked** a day. I could not work for Mr. Robison any longer."[3] Cy went on to say he was no backslider or malingerer, words that meant troublemaker or person faking an illness. It was clear Cy was still angry, and the chance to leave St. Louis was too good to let pass.

On his own, Cy went to Hot Springs to get ready for the 1901 season. While he was there, Mr. Robison told several reporters that Cy had not been loyal to him or the team. He said, "Even Cy Young forgot to be grateful to the man [Mr. Robison] who picked him up out of a country league and gave him a start in life."[4] A sportswriter in St. Louis defended Cy by saying Mr. Robison had made thousands of dollars from the great pitcher. The Spiders had drawn big crowds at League

Portrait of Cy in his Boston Americans uniform, about 1902.

Courtesy of Library of Congress Photo

Park just to see him pitch. Because of that, Mr. Robison had become a rich man and should not have any bad words toward Cy.[5]

Even though Mr. Robison said these things, he still wanted his pitcher to come back to St. Louis. In early April, he asked Chief Zimmer to travel to Hot Springs and have a talk with Cy. Mr. Robison thought that Cy's old catcher and good friend might be able to change his mind and bring him back to St. Louis. At that time, there were no rules against players leaving one league for another or even doing it twice. Despite all the hard words, Mr. Robison still left the door open.

If there was any doubt about where Cy was going, he ended it with a letter to Charles Somers, the team owner in Boston. He wrote, "Please pay no attention to any reports about me jumping my contract. I have signed with the Boston American League club for 1901 and I will play in that city or nowhere." He went on to say he was a man of honor, and once he signed a contract, he would never leave for another team.[6]

By April, many National League players had signed with the new American League, ensuring that the organization would have enough teams to start play in a few weeks. The eight cities with new ball clubs were Boston, Baltimore, Chicago, Cleveland, Detroit, Milwaukee, Philadelphia, and Washington, D.C. The organizers of the American League were sure there were enough rooters in those cities to support their teams. Men like Ban Johnson, president of the new league, and Charles Somers, who owned both the Cleveland and the Boston teams, were sure they could be successful and hold their own against the National League. Soon the baseball world would find out.

DID YOU KNOW?

Of the eight teams that started the American League in 1901, only four are still playing today. They are Boston, Chicago, Cleveland, and Detroit.

SEVEN

THE WORLD SERIES BEGINS

*Young was in wonderfully good form and pitched a
game which could not be excelled.*
    —*Washington Evening Star,* October 1903

THE MANAGER AND third baseman of Cy's new team, the Boston
Americans, was Jimmy Collins, who had also left the National
League for a chance to make a better living. The Americans would
play their home games at the Huntington Avenue Grounds, a new
wooden park that could seat 9,000 rooters. Charles Somers had
bought the land, which at one time had been used for traveling cir-
cuses and carnivals. For some reason, the park had only one entrance
and one **turnstile,** which meant any large crowd would have to wait
a long time to get in. Mr. Somers decided to charge only twenty-five
cents for a grandstand seat, half of what Boston's National League
team charged.

Team photo of the Boston Americans, about 1903. Cy is in the front row, second from the right.

The Boston season began on April 26 at Baltimore, and the Americans had to play ten games away before coming home to their new ballpark. But just as the season began, Cy became sick with tonsillitis. He missed the first game and tried to come back to pitch the next day, but he had to leave in the sixth inning. He was not yet ready to play and gave up ten runs before manager Collins took him out of the game. By early May, Cy was feeling better and struck out seven batters to win 10–2 against Washington.

The Boston home opener was set to be played at 3:00 p.m. against the Philadelphia Athletics. The Americans' train from Washington was hours late, leaving the players only minutes to change into their uniforms and take the field for practice. Even though everyone was hungry, they had to skip lunch in order to get ready for the game.

At thirty-four years old, Cy was about start a new chapter in his baseball career. At that age, most ballplayers were thinking about retiring and going home to live with their families all year round. Cy was different—he still had the strength and energy to pitch like someone ten years younger. He was nowhere close to being finished as a major league star, although his teammates and sportswriters were now calling him "Old Cy."

An hour before game time, the grandstand at Huntington Avenue Grounds was nearly filled with people, many of them waving small American flags. Ropes were put out in center field for the 2,000 rooters unable to get a seat. While the crowd was being settled, a band marched to the infield, playing popular songs of the day. A carriage drawn by four beautiful white horses rode onto the outfield, carrying signs wishing good luck to the team and to the American League.

Before the start of the game, a man holding a **megaphone** stood in front of the grandstand, shouting out the player lineups. This was something new and soon would be used at most of the ballparks. A moment later, the Boston players ran onto the field to the cheers of 11,000 rooters.

Cy did not allow the Philadelphia team to score a run until the eighth inning. By then, Boston was far ahead and beat the Athletics, 12–4. Cy had won Boston's first home opener in the American League, giving all the new rooters a lot to cheer about. Everyone went home happy, knowing the Americans would be one of the better teams.

In late May, the Americans went on another trip away from home, stopping in Cleveland for a weekend series against the Blues, the nickname for the new club. It had been two years since Cy had played at League Park, and the trip there was a real homecoming for him. After the first game on Saturday, Cy went back to the team hotel and sat in the lobby, greeting old friends from his many years in Cleveland. Cy and some of the other Americans took part in a "fanning bee," which was a gathering in the hotel lobby for players and rooters to talk about baseball. The players would answer questions from the rooters about who had the best team or best players and about who might win the pennant. It was a great way to relax and have fun.

Cy had a good time talking with old friends about his years in Cleveland. He told one of the sportswriters, "It never has seemed like the old times since we left here. No town has the rooters that can outdo those of Cleveland when they feel friendly towards the players. I believe I have more friends here today than in any other city."[1]

Cy left Cleveland a cheerful man, having had a chance to meet with some of his oldest friends. There were other reasons to be happy, though, including winning a lot of ball games. Cy began a win streak that went through June and into July. He beat all the teams he pitched against, both the good ones and the not so good. On July 12, Cy won his eleventh straight game, defeating Philadelphia, 5–3. This was the longest victory streak of his career. Four days later, he won again, beating Cleveland in a wild game, 10–8. Even though he had achieved twelve wins in a row, he did not like the way he had pitched against the Blues. He asked manager Collins for another chance against them before the series ended.

Four days later, he faced Cleveland again, with Earl Moore pitching for the Blues. Moore was a young pitcher from Columbus, Ohio, with a good future ahead of him. The game turned out to be a real battle. After nine innings, the score was tied, with only one run for each team. The Americans were not able to score in the top of the tenth, but the Blues got several hits in the bottom of the inning and scored a single run to stop Cy at twelve straight wins.

Though his streak had ended, Cy continued as the best pitcher in the American League. When the season ended, Cy had the most wins in the league with 33 and had allowed fewer than two runs a game! He struck out the most batters with 158 and tied for first place among pitchers with five shutouts. He was second in the number of innings pitched and had started 41 games. For a man who had already passed his thirty-fourth birthday, it was a terrific **feat**.

Boston did not win the pennant, finishing in second place with a 79–57 record, just behind Chicago. Manager Collins had a batting average of .332 and scored 108 runs. First baseman John "Buck" Freeman had 12 home runs, the second most for any player in the league, and 114 runs batted in. The Americans were a great team and were sure to be fighting for the pennant in 1902.

Several days after the season ended, Cy boarded a train for Cleveland with a final stop in Newcomerstown, where he would get on a wagon for the short ride to Gilmore. He talked with the newspapers about the American League's plans to put a team in St. Louis for the 1902 season. Cy believed the club would have plenty of rooters at the games, with old teammates Jesse Burkett and Roderick "Bobby" Wallace signing to play there.

At home in Gilmore, Cy got news that his good friend and catcher Lou Criger was sick with typhoid fever. He and Bobby packed a suitcase, and the two of them left for Elkhart, Indiana, where Lou made his home. Bobby liked to travel with Cy as much as she could.

Cy had suffered from typhoid fever nine years before and had taken a long time to recover. Cy and Bobby stayed with Lou for nearly two weeks until he felt well enough to sit in a chair. Pleased that Lou was doing well, the Youngs returned to Gilmore for Cy to do some hunting before winter. The trip to Elkhart showed what good friends Cy and Bobby could be.

The winter of 1902 turned out to be a busy one. Cy received a letter from Harvard University asking him to coach their pitchers in February and March. Many colleges asked major league ballplayers to coach while they were waiting for spring training to begin. Cy accepted the job, and in February he and Bobby took the train to Boston. They stayed at a hotel, where several reporters were waiting around to ask questions. Cy talked about his new job: "I was somewhat surprised when I was asked to come on and coach the Harvard University candidates. You see, we are so far away from here in Ohio that I did not dream anyone would want me for such work."[2]

Cy did not understand—or he was too modest—but he had a lot of pitching experience to share with the Harvard players. He knew how to throw any pitch and could judge who had the makings of a pitcher and who did not. All this skill helped Cy be a good coach for the Harvard baseball team.

Portrait of Lou Criger, about 1903.
Courtesy of McGreevy Collection, Boston Public Library

The reporters wanted to talk with Bobby about what she thought of Boston. She gave them a pleasant view of the city: "I just love Boston. I fell in love with it last summer when I came here with Mr. Young. It has been so much cooler than St. Louis and there are so many seashore places near."[3]

Cy and Bobby were happy in Boston as coaching season began. Cy had the Harvard pitchers throw to the catchers and then run around the bases four times before heading to the locker room. All of this was done indoors in the college gym. The players had a batting cage to hit in, a place to practice fielding, and a soft area to work on sliding to the bases. A wooden floor was covered with soil to imitate an outdoor playing field.

Cy planned to stay at Harvard until the end of March and then report late to the Americans' spring training camp in Augusta, Georgia. Manager Collins knew Cy always stayed in shape to play and did not worry about him missing part of the training. While working with the college players, Cy did some pitching himself and probably did his share of running. When his coaching job came to an end, he sent word to Collins to expect him in Augusta in the first week of April.

At the start of the season, sports reporters were predicting which teams would be most likely win the pennant, and the Americans were expected to be among them. With Cy pitching there was always a good chance for a championship season.

On April 19, Cy started the opening game against Baltimore. He did not have a great performance, but he hung on to win, 7–6. More than 14,000 rooters had made their way to the Huntington Avenue Grounds for the first day of the season. In addition to being opening day, April 19 was Patriots' Day, a special holiday celebrated in Massachusetts. It was on this day in 1775 that the Revolutionary War had begun: eight long years until England surrendered and America became a free country. In 1894, the city leaders in Boston created a holiday to remember the brave men who fought for independence. It became Patriots' Day, which is still celebrated today.

The rooters in Boston had a day off from work and came out to Huntington Park in large numbers. Luckily, there were now several entrances for people to walk through, which helped the game start on time. Some of the ticket prices were raised to fifty cents, but there were still 3,000 seats on the first-base side for twenty-five cents. The best seats behind home plate cost seventy-five cents to one dollar.

The Americans played good baseball for much of the season, but it was not quite good enough; they finished in third place, behind the champion Philadelphia Athletics and a new team, the St. Louis Browns. In early October, the players of the American League decided to form an All-Star team to travel across the country, all the way to California. They called themselves the All-Americans and planned games in many of the big cities on the way to the West Coast. Before leaving, they scheduled a few games against the Pittsburgh Pirates, the National League champions. Cy, though not a member of the All-Americans, agreed to pitch the October 12 game in Cleveland. Even this late in the year, over 5,000 rooters came to League Park to see Cy pitch against Pittsburgh. Though the Pirates were a hard-hitting team, Cy did not allow a single run, winning the game 1–0. It was a terrific ending to an already great season in which Cy had won thirty-two games, the best of all the pitchers in the American League.

After the game, Cy returned home to Gilmore. He spent his time working on the farm until February, when he accepted a coaching job at Mercer College in Macon, Georgia. Cy probably took this job because the Americans would be training in the same city. In the middle of February, he started chopping wood every day for three weeks until it was time to leave for the south. When he arrived in Macon, he was already in good shape to run and throw with the college players.

Now thirty-six years old, Cy kept up with the Mercer College boys, even though some were just about half his age. An Ohio newspaper joked about Cy's age, writing, "He is now so old that Chicago was a flag station when he started and burgs like Toledo were never thought of."[4] Since these cities were founded in the first half of the nineteenth century, that made Cy about seventy-three-years old, which of course he was not.

In late March, when the Boston team came to Macon to train, they played a game against Mercer College. To make things fair, Cy pitched for the college team and beat the Americans 5–1. It had to be a big thrill for the college boys to play against an American League team and win the game. When Cy was pitching, the team always had a good chance to win.

The Americans returned home to Boston in the middle of April for the start of the 1903 season. On April 20, Cy pitched the opener in front of 19,000 rooters, the largest crowd that ever gathered to see a game in Huntington Avenue Grounds. More than half the people were standing behind the ropes in center and left field, but nobody seemed to mind. After six innings, Boston led 6–0 and looked to have an easy win. In the top of the seventh, though, Cy had big trouble, allowing Philadelphia to score six runs and tie the game. He eventually lost 10–7, a big letdown for opening day.

Four days later, Cy pitched a much better game, beating Philadelphia, 2–1. He faced the Athletics' Eddie Plank, one of the American League's top pitchers. In the upcoming games, Cy had to pitch against tough competition: Charles "Chief" Bender and George "Rube" Waddell of Philadelphia, Jack Chesbro of New York, and Adrian "Addie" Joss of Cleveland. In addition to Cy, the Boston Americans had another top pitcher, Bill Dineen. Every one of these men was much younger than Cy, but he still managed to be the best of them all. His pitching, along with that of Bill Dineen and Tom Hughes, led Boston to the championship of the American League.

The Americans won ninety-one games and lost only forty-seven. They finished far ahead of second-place Philadelphia, winning by an amazing fourteen and a half games. It was a special season in Boston, but the year was not over. The National League champs, the Pittsburgh Pirates, agreed to play Boston in the first-ever World Series!

In the first two years of the American League, there had been no talk of an October series with the National Leaguers. Few people believed the new league had enough good players to compete for an overall championship. By 1903, it had become clear that the American League had excellent teams on the same level as those of the National

70

THE WORLD SERIES THAT ALMOST WASN'T

In the second week of September 1903, Pittsburgh team owner Barney Dreyfuss told the newspapers he wanted to see his team play the Boston Americans to find out who was best. Mr. Dreyfuss said that the series should be nine games and that the players could share the money earned from ticket sales. It was thoughtful of Mr. Dreyfuss to offer all the money to the players and keep none for himself.

Days later Henry Killilea, the new owner of the Americans, agreed that there should be a series but that the two owners should get some of the money themselves. The Boston players thought that the players still would receive at least 75 percent of the ticket sales.

Another week went by, and the Americans were surprised to learn that Mr. Killilea wanted to take half of the ticket sales. The players were angry with the news and told manager Jimmy Collins that they would not play. The team could do this because the Americans' contracts ended September 30, and they did not have to play any more baseball until the next year. The contracts of the Pirates ended October 15, which meant they had no choice but to play.

At the end of the month, there was still no deal. Rooters in both cities worried that the series would not happen. Some of the Boston players packed their suitcases and were ready to leave for their hometowns. At the last minute, a deal was announced in favor of the players. Both teams would get 75 percent of the ticket sales, and the two owners would get the other 25 percent.

League. In early September 1903, Boston had a big lead for first place in the American League, and the Pittsburgh Pirates were number one in the National League. Rooters in many cities, as well as a lot of baseball writers, were demanding a series between the two league winners.

The nine-game series would be played with the first three games in Boston, the next four in Pittsburgh, and the last two in Boston, if needed. The first team to win five games would be the world champion. The agreement allowed the players to take 75 percent of the ticket sales and the two team owners to split the remaining 25 percent.

The opening game of the World Series was set for Thursday, October 1, at 3:00 p.m. An excited crowd of rooters made its way to Huntington Avenue and into the ballpark. The people of Boston behaved much like the Cleveland crowds had at the 1895 Temple Cup. They arrived hours before game time with horns, whistles, and cowbells, and they shouted as loudly as they could. The streetcars brought rooters to the park nonstop for two full hours. A crowd of 16,242 squeezed their way inside the Huntington Avenue Grounds, which could seat only 9,000; the rest had to stand behind the ropes in center and left field. Outside the park, people stood on rooftops to get a view of the game, some of them from as far as a quarter of a mile away.

The Pittsburgh Pirates had some of the best hitters in all of baseball. Cy had to be careful in pitching to Clarence "Ginger" Beaumont, who batted .341; to player-manager Fred Clarke, who had finished second with a .351 average; and to Honus Wagner, the National League batting champion at .355. Wagner was the best shortstop in all of baseball. Pitcher Sam Leever had won twenty-five games and lost only seven. In the opening game, Cy would face another twenty-five-game winner, Charles "Deacon" Phillippe.

The game started quietly, with Cy getting the first two hitters out. Then Tommy Leach, the Pirates' third baseman, drove a triple into the crowd behind the ropes. (Before the game, the umpires had ruled that any ball hit into the ropes was an automatic triple.) That hit seemed to upset Cy, and four runs scored before he could get the third out. The

Pirates stole three bases, and Lou Criger threw a ball into the outfield for a big error. From then on, Cy pitched better but did allow the first-ever World Series home run to outfielder Jimmy Sebring. The Boston rooters went home disappointed, as the Americans lost the first game, 7–3. The next day, although the skies were dark and rain seemed likely, the game went on. Bill Dineen pitched a super game, and Pat Dougherty hit two home runs, leading Boston to a 3–0 win and tying the series at one game each.

By Saturday at noon, thousands of rooters had lined up outside the park. The World Series had gotten off to a thrilling start, and now a crowd of more than 20,000 rooters was trying to get tickets. At 2:00 p.m., after 18,000 of them had been admitted, the ticket office closed because the business manager was worried that so many people would be standing in the outfield that they might interfere with the game.

The rooters kept pushing at the outfield ropes, trying to make more room to stand. Suddenly, the ropes broke, and hundreds of rooters ran along the first and third base lines, forming a big "U" around the outside of the bases and home plate. The policemen on duty tried to push the rooters back, but there were not enough officers to make any difference. They called for help, and seventy more policemen ran to the park. They started swinging baseball bats at the crowd, and within a few minutes everybody had moved back behind the quickly repaired ropes.

At the same time, several thousand boys and men ran right past the ticket windows and onto the field without paying! With all the attention on the police and the crowd, nobody in the office saw the extra people sneaking in.

Modern-day ballparks seat anywhere from 31,000 to 56,000 people. Imagine if you went to a game and twice that number tried to push their way inside. That would be 62,000 to 112,000 people! Today, rooters are never allowed on the field, and only a small number of standing room tickets are sold. The wild scene at Huntington Park could not happen nowadays, but in 1903, the American and National League

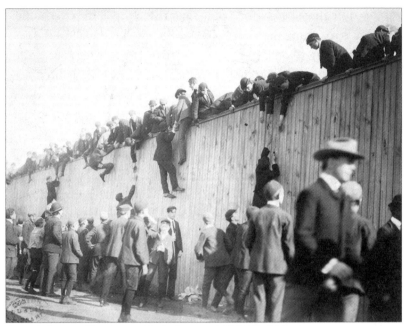

Crowd photo at Huntington Park, Boston, 1903 World Series.
Courtesy of McGreevy Collection, Boston Public Library

teams were looking to make as much money as they could and did not care much about the safety of the crowd. Today, safety is the most important concern.

Tom Hughes started the game for Boston against Deacon Phillippe, who had only one day to rest. Because Cy also had pitched on Thursday, he had the day off and was not expected to enter the game. In the third inning, though, Hughes gave up three runs, and a call went to Cy to get dressed and take to the mound. He hit Honus Wagner with his first pitch but stopped Pittsburgh from then on. Cy finished the game, pitching seven strong innings, but the Americans were not able to rally against Deacon Phillippe and lost 4–2. The Pirates led the series, two games to one.

On Sunday morning, the Americans boarded a train for Pittsburgh to reach the Pirates' Exposition Park on Monday morning. Traveling along with the team were the "Royal Rooters," a group of about 150

Photo of the Boston Americans and Pittsburgh Pirates teams during the 1903 World Series. Cy is in the second row, sixth from the left.

Courtesy of McGreevy Collection, Boston Public Library

people led by Mike McGreevy, a saloon owner and the most enthusiastic rooter in all of Boston. The men were ready to cheer loudly at all four games in Pittsburgh, willing to compete with the thousands of Pirates rooters sure to be at the games.

Monday morning came with dark clouds and rain. The grounds became too wet to play on, and the game was canceled. The rained-out game allowed all the pitchers to rest their arms at least one more day.

The weather on Tuesday was better, good enough for the fourth game to be played. When the Americans walked onto the field, a group of rooters in the right-field seats stood up and yelled for Cy. The men were from Cleveland and had not seen Cy since his days with the Spiders. They had come all the way from Ohio in hope of seeing their old friend on the mound again.

The pitchers for game four were Bill Dineen for the Americans and Deacon Phillippe for the Pirates. Manager Clarke had to use Deacon again for the third straight game because Sam Leever had a sore arm and was not able to play. Even though Deacon was tired, he had a 2–1 lead after six innings. The Pirates added three runs in the seventh inning, building the lead to 5–1.

The Americans had one more chance in the top of the ninth. They scored three runs and then loaded the bases with only one out. Manager Collins decided to have two **pinch hitters,** one for Lou Criger and one for Bill Dineen. Neither pinch hitter got a hit, sending easy fly balls to the outfield. Pittsburgh won the game and needed only two more wins for the championship. The Americans were in deep trouble, but they still had Cy to pitch the next game.

On Wednesday, October 7, Cy was ready to begin his third game in just seven days—the most important game of the series. If Cy lost, the Americans would be down four games to one, with the next two games still in Pittsburgh. The Pirates would need to win only one of those two to become champions.

Minutes before the game, a man came up to Lou Criger and promised to give him $12,000 if he would make sure that Boston would not win that afternoon. Why? The man had bet another person $50,000 that Pittsburgh would win game five. In the early 1900s, betting on baseball games was a popular form of gambling. People would meet outside ballparks or in saloons and bet money on who would win that day's game. Newspapers even wrote stories about who was betting and how much.

But this was different, because the man who promised Lou money had asked him to make sure the Americans lost. This was called **"fixing"** a game, which was a crime. He wanted Lou to let Cy's pitches get past him when there were Pirates on base or to throw the ball wildly when a Pittsburgh player was trying to steal. Lou, being an honest man, refused the offer and told Cy, and later the president of the American League, what had happened. Cy, like Lou, believed in playing an honest game and would not listen to anyone trying to "fix" a game.

Long after Cy had retired, he told a sportswriter that gamblers also had visited him in Pittsburgh and offered him $20,000 if he would pitch poorly and let Pittsburgh win.[5] They asked him not to throw as hard as he usually did and to walk a lot of the Pirate batters. Cy refused.

If Cy and Lou had agreed to let Pittsburgh win and if people had found out later, it might have ruined the entire American League. Both might have lost their jobs and not been allowed to play major league baseball ever again. Rooters would think that the league and the players were dishonest and would not buy tickets to the games. Without rooters, the team owners would not be able to pay their players, and the league might have gone out of business.

The Americans needed a great game from Cy, and that was what they got. Cy was at his best, allowing not a single run until the eighth inning. Boston scored a total of ten runs in the sixth and seventh innings to give Cy a big lead. He did not walk a batter, and he gave up just six hits, winning 11–2.

The Royal Rooters were sitting in the grandstand just behind the Americans' bench. During the game, they sang loudly to cheer on the players. For no real reason, they chose the song "Tessie," from a popular Broadway musical.

The song probably did not matter to Cy, but he pitched so well that the rooters kept on singing. The words of the song were:

> *Tessie, you make me feel so badly;*
> *Why don't you turn around.*
> *Tessie, you know I love you madly;*
> *Babe, my heart weighs about a pound.*

A few of the men decided to change the words a little to make fun of the Pittsburgh players. When Honus Wagner came to bat, the Royal Rooters sang as loudly as they could:

> *Honus, why do you hit so badly,*
> *Take a seat and sit down.*
> *Honus, at bat you look so sadly,*
> *Hey, why don't you get out of town.*

Royal Rooters at the 1903 World Series.
Courtesy of McGreevy Collection, Boston Public Library

After several innings of the constant singing, some of the Pirates were so annoyed that they lost concentration. Usually, players don't pay attention to what is being sung or yelled from the grandstand. They can block out the noise and pay complete attention to the game. Years later, Tommy Leach, the Pirates third baseman, talked about the Royal Rooters and "Tessie" in a baseball book called *The Glory of Their Times.* Tommy hated the song and thought it helped Boston in the series.[6]

With Cy's fine game, the Americans trailed Pittsburgh three games to two. Manager Collins told the newspapers that Cy would pitch again on Friday and then, if needed, in game nine in Boston. Bill Dineen started game six and won, 6–3. With the series now even, Cy had the chance to put Boston ahead before the two teams left Pittsburgh.

After an extra day off because of rain and cold, Cy pitched once more against Deacon Phillippe. More than 17,000 Pittsburgh rooters came out to Exposition Park, the second-largest crowd ever to fit into

Portrait of Jimmy Collins of the Boston Americans.

the grounds. Just as in Boston, many of the people stood behind ropes in the outfield. The Americans hit a bunch of baseballs into the standing crowd that went for triples and helped them take a 6–2 lead into the seventh inning. Cy struck out six batters in the game to lead Boston to a 7–3 victory and break the tie. Now it was the Americans who had to win only one more game, and it would be played in Boston.

Cy and his teammates hurried back to their hotel for a quick dinner and then caught a 7:00 p.m. train to Boston. As the Americans left the hotel, the Royal Rooters were in the lobby leading cheers for every member of the team. The heroes were Cy and Bill Dineen, who had won three of the four games at Exposition Park and made sure that the series went back to Boston.

Once again, bad weather forced the teams to cancel the Monday game. This was bad news for the Royal Rooters, who had hired a band to play and had been promised seats right on the field, between the two teams' benches. The next day the weather was cold but good enough to play, and the Rooters happily walked on field and took their prized seats.

Bill Dineen pitched against Deacon Phillippe, who was starting his fifth game in the series. That was too much to ask for any pitcher, but Deacon tried as hard as he could to win another for Pittsburgh. He gave up only three runs, but Bill Dineen was even better, allowing not a single Pirate to cross home plate. Boston won 3–0, and the first World Series belonged to the Americans!

After the game, sportswriters talked to most of the players. Cy was pleased with his team, saying, "I knew we would win. I knew the Boston Americans team, in fair condition would beat any ball team in the country."[7] He was right, as his team showed the baseball world that they were the best in America. Most people now agreed that the two leagues were equal, even though the American League was only three years old.

Henry Killilea, the Boston owner, told the newspapers that the eight games had earned $70,000 for the players and owners. He believed that the Americans would each get a check for around $1,800.

Team photo of the Boston Americans, about 1903. Cy is standing in the second row, third from the left.

Courtesy of McGreevy Collection, Boston Public Library

That was a large share for the men, some of whom earned that amount for a full season! Cy made around twice that much each year but was surely grateful to take the extra money home for the winter.

What a year it was. Cy now had a world championship victory to go along with a Temple Cup win in Cleveland. If he had wanted to retire and take care of his farm, most people would have given him a big round of applause. But Cy was far from done with baseball.

DID YOU KNOW?

In 1902, the average American worker earned $700 per year or about $14 a week. To spend a dollar or two of that to see a baseball game was a big expense. Most people had to be careful with their money, buying the twenty-five-cent seats rather than the dollar ones.

EIGHT

CY IS PERFECT

*Nothing like swinging an ax or working the crosscut
saw on trees to keep in condition during the winter.*

—Cy Young (Cy Young files, National Baseball Hall
of Fame and Museum)

C Y CAME BACK home, this time to Peoli, a small village next to
Gilmore where he and Bobby had bought their own farm, a large
one of 160 acres. With his World Series check, Cy had a lot of money to
invest in the farm and plenty left over. It surely was a happy time for
Mr. and Mrs. Young, as Cy was still the best pitcher in baseball and had
earned a good living for many years. Everywhere he went, people rec-
ognized him and wanted to shake his hand. There were few places Cy
could go without someone yelling, "That's Cy Young!"

While Cy was home in Peoli, a Cleveland newspaper published an
article on why he had been able to have such a long baseball career and
such a happy life: "He is a gentleman. He is never guilty of rowdyism.
He hasn't found it necessary to accumulate a stock of bad habits in
order to have a good time."[1] The story mentioned that Cy never drank

much alcohol and made sure that he lived a clean, healthy life. Sports-writers and baseball fans thought highly of him, both on and off the field.

The calendar soon turned to February, and that meant another trip to Hot Springs, Arkansas. Cy was starting his fifteenth year of major league baseball, an amazing feat for any player. A Cleveland newspaper wrote about Cy's wonderful career: "When one considers that great old Cy has been in the big leagues for fifteen years, the great-est praise must be bestowed upon him. Five or six years in the fast company [the major leagues] is more than most of the pitchers get, but here is a man who was a star fifteen years ago and has pitched the same kind of ball every year since."[2]

The newspaper articles were a good study of why Cy had excelled in major league baseball. He had taken great care to do all the right things to keep himself in condition, more so than a lot of his fellow ballplayers. Even though he was thirty-six years old, Cy still had some good years of baseball left in him.

On April 14, 1904, Boston opened the season at New York. They already had won a pennant and the first World Series. What more could they do? Well, the Americans were determined to win another pennant and play in a second World Series.

Cy faced Jack Chesbro, the best pitcher for the Highlanders. New York scored five runs in the first inning and went on to win 8–2. Five days later Cy pitched his first game at Boston, winning 3–2 in front of another crowd standing behind the ropes. Cy must have been glad to walk to the pitcher's mound and see the blue-and-white "World Cham-pions" flag flying behind him near the center-field wall. Next to it was a red flag for the champions of the American League. The rest of the teams in the American League would try to take those titles away, but Cy and his teammates were ready to defend them.

Near the end of April, Cy pitched two more games, losing the first 2–0 to Philadelphia and winning the second 4–1 over Washington. In that first game, Cy gave up two runs in the first inning but nothing more for the rest of the game. In his victory against Washington, Cy entered the game in the third inning, with Boston leading 3–1, and did not allow any runs to the Senators. Over the two games, Cy had pitched a total of fourteen innings in a row without allowing a single run.

His next start was at home against the Philadelphia Athletics. The pitcher facing him was Rube Waddell, whom many thought could throw even harder and better than Cy. The spring weather felt more like summer, and many rooters took off their coats and rolled up their sleeves to try to cool off. The battle between two great pitchers began.

Neither team was able to score a run through the first five innings. Cy pitched to fifteen batters, and none of them reached first base. In the sixth inning, Boston got the game's first run, while Philadelphia still had not put a single runner on base. Two more Boston runs came in the seventh, giving Cy a 3–0 lead. The rooters in the grandstand looked at their scorecards and saw that Cy had gotten out twenty-one straight batters. They started cheering loudly with every pitch he threw, hoping to see a no-hit, no-run game.

There had been a no-hitter in the American League back in 1902 by Jimmy Callahan of the Chicago White Sox. He had pitched a wonderful game but walked two batters, and the Chicago fielders made three errors to let runners on base. This game was different because Cy had not walked anybody, and the Boston infielders and outfielders had not made a single error.

Philadelphia batted in the eighth, but all three men went back to the bench without a hit or walk. Only three more outs to go! By now, in the ninth inning, almost every rooter in the park was standing up. The first Philadelphia hitter struck out, and the second hit an easy ground ball for out number two. The last batter for Cy was Rube Waddell. In today's games, no manager would let a pitcher bat at such an important time. They are usually the weakest hitters on the team. But this was 1904, and managers, for the most part, just let the pitcher try to hit. Everyone in the ballpark took a deep breath as Cy went into his **windup** and threw. Rube took a big swing and hit a fly ball to center field. Charles "Chick" Stahl moved a few steps, stopped, and made the catch. Cy Young had pitched a no-hit, no-run, nobody-on-base game! Now we call it a **perfect game**, but in 1904 there was no real word for it.

The rooters climbed out of the grandstands and ran onto the field to shake hands with Cy. One excited man reached in his wallet and gave Cy money. The no-hit pitcher did not need it but smiled and put the bill in his pocket. Chick Stahl ran by and gave the game-winning baseball to Cy, who would later take it home to Peoli.

Sportswriters asked Cy what he thought, and he said, "I did my best to win. I was in perfect shape and the hot weather just suited me. I am glad for the sake of the Boston fans, who have given me such loyal support."[3] Soon the reporters were checking the old records to see when another pitcher had set down twenty-seven straight batters in nine innings. They found only two games, both of which had taken place in 1880, twenty-four years earlier.

Newspapers all throughout the United States printed stories about Cy's rare feat and called him "King of the Pitchers." He was able to do things in baseball that few pitchers could match. He could win thirty games a year, win a World Series, and pitch every three days—or even every day or two, if needed.

Cy's next start was against the Detroit Tigers. The game was scoreless through the seventh inning, when Cy finally allowed a base hit. The scoreless game went to the fifteenth inning, when the Americans scored a single run. Cy got the Tigers out one more time, and the game was his, 1–0. He had now gone thirty-eight innings without giving up a run. In just two games he had pitched twenty-four innings—almost the same as pitching three complete games.

On May 17, the Cleveland Blues were in Boston to face Cy. For seven innings he was as tough as ever, not giving up a single run. In the top of the eighth, the Blues finally broke the streak, scoring three runs and winning the game 3–1. The streak was over, but Cy had made it to forty-five scoreless innings. Cy had set another record, one that would last until 1910. More than a hundred years later, Cy is still tied for eighth place on the all-time list of scoreless innings, a terrific achievement for any pitcher.

As the 1904 season went on, the Americans showed that they were still the best team around, winning the pennant for the second straight year. They had an even better record than the year before, with ninety-five wins and only fifty-nine losses. Cy won twenty-six games, had a career high of ten shutouts, and allowed fewer than two runs per game. He and his teammates got ready for another World Series, this time against the New York Giants, who were the champions of the National League. But to the great disappointment of baseball rooters everywhere, the Giants manager, John McGraw, refused to play.

McGraw gave long stories to the newspapers, trying to explain why he turned down the chance to play Boston, but few people understood his reasons. Because of his selfishness, there was no World Series in 1904. Cy lost a chance to play for another championship and to make extra money for him and Bobby. The 1903 World Series victory would be the only one for him in his long baseball career.

In March 1905, Cy made his yearly trip to Hot Springs, Arkansas. For one of the first times, he had gained a lot of weight over the winter and needed the exercise and hot baths to lose some pounds. From all reports, he quickly got into playing shape and was ready for his sixteenth year in professional baseball. At Hot Springs, in addition to practicing with his Boston teammates, he joined the Cleveland pitchers and catchers in their workouts. Bill Bernhard, one of the Cleveland men, spoke to the papers about Cy: "When the rest of us pitchers report to Hot Springs, we act if those arms of ours were made of glass. But not so with 'Old' Cy. The very first day he cut loose as if he had been pitching all winter."[4]

Most sportswriters thought Boston would win a third pennant and remain at the top for at least another season. But the year did not turn out that way for Cy and the Americans. They did not win the pennant or even come close. Cy had an incredibly low ERA of 1.82 but still lost more games than he won, and rooters began to think that his career might be finished. He was thirty-eight years old, and it made sense that the end might finally have come.

The following year, 1906, Cy had one of his worst seasons, winning only thirteen games and losing twenty-one. The Americans had played badly, finishing in last place. Rooters were even more convinced that their great star had reached the end of the line.

Despite all the bad talk, Cy refused to listen. In 1907, he proved he could still pitch, winning twenty-one games, though the Americans moved up only one place in the standings, to seventh. The next year, Cy won another twenty-one games and lost only eleven with an ERA of 1.26, the lowest of his career.

Though Cy was winning, he pitched fewer innings and rested his arm more than he had in past seasons. But there were still many times when Cy looked like the same pitcher he had been ten years before. On June 30, 1908, the Americans were in New York to face the Highlanders. Cy pitched carefully to lead-off batter Harry Niles but walked him. As Niles stood at first base, he thought Cy was not watching him closely and tried to steal second. Lou Criger made a perfect throw to second, and Niles became the first out of the game. Cy got the next two batters out to end the first inning.

While the Boston hitters scored a total of eight big runs, Cy actually needed only one as he put down the next twenty-four New York batters for another no-hitter. Cy had pitched another no-hit, no-run, no-base-runner game, coming as close as possible to what he had done in 1904. Only that walk to Harry Niles had spoiled another perfect game.

Later in the season, the Americans planned a day at Huntington Park to honor Cy for everything he had done for the team since 1901. They chose August 13 because none of the American League teams had a game scheduled for that day, which meant an All-Star team could be chosen to play an exhibition game against Boston.

By game time, about 20,000 fans (the new name for rooters) had pushed their way inside the park, all of them wanting to say thanks to

Cy. There were several speeches in Cy's honor and three large silver **loving cups** as gifts. The first was from the players of the American League, the second from the Boston newspapers, and the third from Cy's many friends. After the game, John Taylor, the Boston team owner, gave the total of the ticket sales to Cy: nearly $7,000! In today's money, that is just about $170,000.

Since the game was just for fun, the Americans all wore silly costumes, like a clown, a cowboy, a navy admiral, and Uncle Sam. Cy himself walked to the pitcher's mound wearing a large straw hat and farmer's clothes. While the fans had a good laugh, Cy pitched two innings, then left for the bench as everyone gave him a loud cheer.

When the season came to an end, Cy packed his bag and left for Peoli. He would be busy in October, pitching a game for Newcomerstown on the twelfth. This game was a chance for Cy and other local players to earn extra money from the ticket sales. A crowd of 2,500 people was there to welcome him home. Many of the people at the ballpark were farmers taking a break from the fall harvest to see their neighbor Cy pitch. He won the game easily, 11–3.

While Cy was still in Boston, plans had been made to have a "Cy Young Day" in Ohio on October 24, with a charity game to benefit the new Union Hospital being built to serve the people in and around Tuscarawas County. Cy was excited about the day and raising money for the new medical clinic. He told the organizers of the game that he would pay for a large room in the hospital. It was a bighearted thing to do, but Cy was full of pride about where he lived and wanted to help as much as he could.

The day of the game arrived, and the weather was in the upper sixties, perfect for a late fall afternoon. More than 4,000 people bought tickets to see Cy play ball. When he came to bat for the first time, the crowd gave him a long cheer that lasted several minutes. On the pitcher's mound, Cy struck out batters all afternoon, and his team had no trouble in winning 4–1. That night, there was a party for Cy in Newcomerstown. A hundred people attended and gave him another silver loving cup. By

Cy holding a trophy from Cy Young Day, Boston, 1908.

the end of the night, a great amount of money had been raised for the new Union Hospital, thanks to Cy and the people around him.

In early December, Cy was working on the farm when he got the news his favorite catcher and good friend Lou Criger had been traded to the St. Louis Browns. The two men had been teammates since the old days in the 1890s with the Cleveland Spiders. Lou and Cy had worked well together for many seasons, probably the best pitcher-catcher team in all of baseball.

Before the season began, the manager of the St. Louis team asked Cy what he thought about the trade. Cy started to walk away but turned around and said, "That's a sore subject with me. I had an idea that you were trying to get me started, so I ducked."[5] Cy knew he had to move on and find another catcher, but the idea that Lou was gone still bothered him quite a bit.

At the beginning of 1909, rumors began to spread that Boston was thinking about trading Cy. The fans in Boston started to get worried, causing manager Fred Lake to tell the newspapers, "I want it under-stood we will never trade Cy unless he expresses a desire to go. In the first place I believe Cy would quit baseball if he was traded to some club he did not like."[6] That stopped the rumors for a short time, but soon the owners of the Chicago Cubs and Chicago White Sox told sportswriters they would pay a big price to get Cy on their team. Cy had little to say about all the talk and made sure to sign his 1909 contract and send it to Boston.

Early on a cold February morning, the phone rang, getting Cy out of his bed to answer. A Cleveland newspaper was calling to ask him if he knew about the trade that had just happened, sending him to Cleveland for two pitchers and $12,500. Cy told the paper, "I have heard nothing about the trade. Of course, the whole thing is up to Mr. Taylor and Mr. Somers [the Cleveland owner]. If they want me for the Cleveland club, I can see no objection to my playing there."[7]

Before long, Mr. Somers called to tell Cy that he was once again a member of the Cleveland ball club, now called the Naps. He took the news well, having started his career in that city and having had many fine years there. He would no longer need to make the long trip to Boston, instead traveling the short distance from Peoli to Cleveland. Cy looked forward to seeing old friends again and visiting with his younger brother Jesse, who worked for a telephone company in downtown Cleveland.

In 1908, the Cleveland team had finished in second place, just behind the Detroit Tigers. They had a good pitching staff, with stars Addie Joss and Bob Rhoads. Adding Cy helped the team's chances for another try at the pennant. Many of the sportswriters thought the Naps were one of the best teams in the American League.

At the end of February, Cy took a train to Cleveland, meeting with Charles Somers to talk about plans for the new season. Cy wore a fancy green suit with a green hat, hardly looking like a farmer from Peoli.

A few weeks later, he left for Mobile, Alabama, to begin workouts with the other Cleveland pitchers. On March 29, Cy and his teammates celebrated his forty-second birthday. He received **telegrams** from Cleveland, Boston, and other American League cities. Cy told the Cleveland sportswriters he could not wait for the season to begin.

Adding to all the excitement, everyone knew that Cy had won a grand total of 478 games in his career. For a long time, it had been thought no major league pitcher could ever win 500, but Cy was closing in on the impossible number. With a good year in Cleveland, he had a chance to reach it.

On April 15, Cy and the Naps were in St. Louis for the opening series. Cy pitched the second game against his old teammates, Lou Criger and Bobby Wallace. Lou got two hits off Cy, but Cleveland scored four times, and Cy held on for his first win of the year, 4–3. After the game, the two friends met in Cy's hotel and talked for several hours.

Eight days later, the team held "Cy Young Day" for the home opener at League Park, but the weather was miserable. The temperature was below fifty degrees, much better for football than baseball. Mr. Somers had hoped for 9,000 to 10,000 fans to welcome Cy, but because of the cold weather only 5,334 were in the grandstands. St. Louis won the game 3–1 to spoil the afternoon for Cy and the Cleveland fans.

The 1909 season did not go as planned. The Naps were losing more than winning, and they finished all the way back in sixth place. During the season, player-manager Nap Lajoie had quit the managing part of the job, and James "Deacon" McGuire took his place. Cy was one of the few Cleveland players to have a good year, winning nineteen games and losing fifteen. He had a strong chance to win twenty games, but in mid-September, McGuire decided to give Cy a rest and to try out some new pitchers from the minor leagues. Cy finished the year with a career total of 497 wins.

In early October, another benefit for the Union Hospital was planned. Cy, being a good neighbor and always willing to help, agreed to pitch again to support the hospital. This time he pitched four strong innings without allowing a run.

Besides helping the Union Hospital raise money, Cy kept busy trying to save the Peoli post office. There had been talk that the office

CY AND HIS CHICKENS

In December 1909, Cy showed off his Rhode Island Reds at a fair in Youngstown, Ohio. Cy had raised chickens for many years and was asked to put them on display. He was not the only baseball player expected to be there: Honus Wagner, still with the Pittsburgh Pirates, entered his Plymouth Rock chickens, and Nap Lajoie, Cy's teammate in Cleveland, was to bring his Leghorns. All the chickens were known to be excellent for laying eggs that the farmers could sell to their local markets. The fair organizers hoped to attract a big crowd because of the three great Major League stars scheduled to appear.

would be closed because so few people lived in the area, and it did not make sense to keep it open. Cy and forty other men signed a letter and sent it to Washington, D.C., asking the government to keep the post office from closing. They knew that Peoli was a very small town, but if there was no post office, the people would have to go to Newcomerstown, much too far to walk. The letter must have worked, because the office stayed open for many years.

Even with all those things to do, Cy still found time to work on the farm until the start of spring training. The 1910 season was going to be different for him, since the Naps were bringing up some young players from the minor leagues, and they were not expected to contend for the pennant. One thing was for sure, though: Cy would have his chance to win his 500th game.

DID YOU KNOW?

When forty-one-year-old Cy pitched his no-hitter in 1908, he was the oldest pitcher in the major leagues to do so. His record would last an amazing eighty-two years until 1990, when forty-three-year-old Nolan Ryan threw a no-hitter for the Texas Rangers.

NINE

A NEW RECORD

Cy was a wonderful guy.
—Ty Cobb (Cy Young files, National Baseball Hall of Fame and Museum

O N APRIL 21, 1910, Cy pitched the Cleveland home opener against the Detroit Tigers. What made the day really special was the completely rebuilt League Park. Mr. Somers had constructed a second level to the grandstand, adding another 9,000 seats and doubling the total to 18,000. At the 1891 opening of the park, Cy had the honor of pitching the very first game. It was hard to believe, but nineteen years later, he was doing the same thing again. Cy did not pitch well and lost to the Tigers, 5–0, before the largest crowd ever for a Naps home opener.

The first part of the year was tough for Cy. In early May, his tonsils began to bother him again, so much so that he went to a Cleveland hospital and had an operation to remove them. He took some time to recover, then returned to pitching, but still did not have much luck. On

Cy with the Cleveland Naps, about 1910.
Courtesy of the National Baseball Hall of Fame and Museum, Cooperstown, NY

June 4, playing against Washington, Cy came to bat against Walter Johnson, a young pitcher who had a fastball as good as Cy's—or even better. Johnson took his windup and threw a hard one that hit Cy in the right shoulder. It had to hurt, but Cy kept on pitching until the seventh inning, when the shoulder became too painful to keep going.

Cy sat on the bench for a week and a half until his arm felt good enough to pitch again. He lost a game to New York, but on June 21 he won his first game of the year. He had to go twelve innings for the 3–2 win against Chicago. Cy looked like his old self, ready to have another good season and to reach his goal of 500 wins. While he looked ahead, New York came to town, and with them catcher Lou Criger, who had been traded from the Browns. Cy went to visit his old pal, but Lou was not feeling well. He had terrible pains in his stomach and had a hard time standing straight up. Cy called the Naps' team doctor and made sure he got Lou to the hospital for an examination. The doctor checked him carefully and discovered that Lou had **appendicitis.** Cy's concern for Lou may have saved his life, and Lou recovered in the hospital until he felt well enough to rejoin the New York team.

On Tuesday, July 19, the Naps were in Washington for a doubleheader. Cy started the second game with only one goal in mind: to get his 500th win. In the first inning, Washington scored a run and held the lead until the top of the ninth inning. Cleveland rallied to score two runs and give Cy the lead with Washington batting in the bottom of the ninth. The Senators fought back with two hits and a fly ball to tie the game at two and load the bases with only one out. While the fans stood up, a determined Cy got the next two batters out and sent the game to extra innings.

Neither team scored in the tenth, but one inning later, the Naps bunched together some hits and pushed across three runs for a 5–2 lead. Though he was tired, Cy put out the Senators in the bottom of the eleventh and history was made: Cy Young had won 500 games! Newspapers across the country printed stories about the win and listed highlights from Cy's long career. No other active pitcher in the American or National leagues had even 300 victories! Christy Mathewson, a great star for the New York Giants, was second with 251. Cy's record still stands today and probably never will be broken.

Sportswriters throughout America stopped calling him "Old Cy" and now referred to him as "Grand Old Man." Everyone was amazed at how he had pitched for more than twenty years and yet still could win games. Cy had a couple of reasons. He said, "There are two things that have enabled me to pitch as long as I have. I pitch no wide curve balls and I have my arm rubbed carefully after every game I pitch."[1] Cy thought trying to make a curveball break too sharply would hurt his arm and shorten his career.

Another reason why Cy was able to keep pitching was good exercise. When the farm chores were done, he often ran three miles in heavy clothing. Running is a great way to exercise, but most people do it wearing shorts and a T-shirt. Imagine running three miles through woods and forests in a coat, pants, and heavy shoes. Cy was way ahead of everybody else.

After some time, all the talk about 500 wins went away, and Cy concentrated on pitching. He had seven victories for the season and ten losses. Though it was not a great year, he told Mr. Somers he would return in good shape for 1911.

At the start of the season, Cy and the Naps received terrible news. Addie Joss, Cy's close friend and roommate in Cleveland, had become seriously ill and died at home in Toledo at the age of thirty-one. Cy was shaken by the news, telling reporters, "My baseball experience has thrown me with practically every man in the big leagues for more than twenty years, but I never met a fairer or squarer man than Addie."[2]

The funeral took place on April 17, with nearly all the Cleveland Naps attending. Plans were made for a benefit game to raise money for Addie's widow, Lillian Joss. On July 24, the Naps played against a group of All-Stars from the American League. When the Naps ran onto the field to start the game, nobody in the grandstand was surprised to see forty-four-year-old Cy Young ready to pitch. Once again, Cy was there to help a friend.

Though Cy continued to pitch, Mr. Somers wanted to see what his new pitchers could do, mostly the ones who were in their twenties. It seemed as though it would never happen, but the time had come for Cy to be given his release from the Cleveland Naps. He took the news well, saying to the papers, "I've not a kick coming. I have been treated finely by the Cleveland club and the fans of the game. I shall stick to baseball as I feel there are a few years of good pitching in the old whip [arm]."[3]

Offers soon came his way from minor league teams hoping to build up attendance when Cy pitched. A team in Lynn, Massachusetts, not far from Boston, offered Cy $100 a game and a chance to own part of the club. Soon after that, the Boston Rustlers of the National League asked Cy to join them for the rest of the season. Always happy in Boston, Cy agreed to travel back east and keep playing baseball.

The Rustlers were the worst team in the league, in last place with no chance of moving up. Cy did what he could, even pitching a 1–0 shutout in September against the Pittsburgh Pirates. He made his last start of the season on October 6 in Brooklyn. With one out in the seventh inning, the Brooklyn batters gave Cy a real beating with eight straight hits. He was taken out of the game for another pitcher, one of the few times that had happened in his career. Boston lost the ball game by a bad score of 13–3. That was not how Cy wanted to finish the year, but he accepted the one-sided loss and began thinking about 1912.

At home for the winter, Cy took care of the farm with the help of his brother-in-law, Fred Miller. He now had three hundred sheep to look after, along with his chickens and cattle. Even as busy as he was with the farm, he still made time for others. When Bobby asked him to help, he agreed to join a group of neighbors in building a home for the new pastor of the nearby Peoli Church. Bobby was a thoughtful person who liked to help her friends and neighbors.

On February 24, 1912, Cy packed his traveling bags for another trip to Hot Springs. One of his neighbors came by with a horse and wagon for the twelve-mile journey to the Newcomerstown train station. All along the way, his many friends stood by the road to wish him luck for the new season. For years, it had been almost a holiday when Cy left home for Hot Springs. The people of Peoli and the other small towns stopped their farm chores to wave to Cy and yell a few words to him.

Through March and early April, Cy practiced with the Boston team, now called the Braves. He believed that he had enough strength left in him for at least one more good year. It really came as a surprise when, just before opening day, his right arm began to hurt. He tried to rest, but no matter what he did, the arm did not get any better. In May, still unable to pitch, he left Boston for Peoli to rest his injured arm.

In August, while still at home, Cy tried to pitch a few innings in Columbus for the Franklin College team. He got only to the third inning, when his arm began hurting too much to go any further. He shouted to the crowd that he was sorry but had to stop right there. That was the last time Cy Young ever pitched in an organized baseball game. For twenty-two years, Cy had been a great major league pitcher. He had won 511 games, lost 315, made 2,803 strikeouts, and allowed an average of fewer than three runs per game. Cy had pitched the Cleveland Spiders to a Temple Cup victory and helped the Boston Americans win the first-ever World Series. Now it was time to say goodbye.

After Cy retired in 1912, other pitchers like Walter Johnson and Joe Wood came along to take his place. It was time for the newer ballplayers to have their chance, and that was okay with Cy. He had never asked for all the attention, and he was glad to be back with Bobby and his hometown friends. That was enough for the "Grand Old Man."

DID YOU KNOW?

Cy played for five different teams in his long major league career: the Cleveland Spiders, the St. Louis Perfectos, and the Boston Braves in the National League and the Boston Americans and Cleveland Naps of the American League.

TEN

THE HALL OF FAME CALLS

I was always happy when I was around him.
—Jane Benedum (Cy Young files, National Baseball
Hall of Fame and Museum

IN 1913, FOR the first springtime since the 1880s, Cy did not get ready to play a summer of baseball. Instead he became a full-time farmer, spending most of his time at home in Peoli. He spent many evenings sitting in his parlor with Bobby, reading the newspaper or one of the books in his library. There were shelves filled with loving cups and baseballs, including the one he used when he got his 500th win.

In the fall and winter, Cy would leave for Jones, Michigan, where Lou Criger had a home in the country near Bair Lake. They and a few of their old Boston teammates went hunting in the forest and fishing in the lake. They told stories and let each other know how they were doing and what they thought about baseball today. Whether they brought back a deer or caught some fish wasn't important; their long-time friendships were what mattered.

Cy at home splitting logs, about 1925.

Cy and his friends were pleased when the American and National Leagues featured "Old-Timers Day" at the ballparks. Teams would invite retired players to take part in a three-inning game for the fans who had not seen their favorite stars in many years. Cy gladly accepted invitations to different baseball parks and would walk to the mound, wave to the crowd, and pitch to a few batters.

On September 8, 1930, Cy played at a special benefit game in Boston at Braves Field. Many onetime Boston players were invited to play against a team of retired stars. Along with Cy were some of his fellow 1903 Boston Americans World Series champs, including Bill Dineen, Jimmy Collins, and Buck Freeman, and an old **rival,** Pittsburgh's Fred Clarke.

The benefit was to raise money for Boston Children's Hospital and for retired ballplayers who needed help with medical bills and everyday living. One of those was Cy's old friend, Lou Criger. For some time, Lou had been terribly sick with **tuberculosis.** Lou's doctor had sent him to Arizona, where the air was cleaner and easier to breathe. Because of his serious illness, Lou was too weak make the trip to Boston.

Many retired ballplayers had a hard time after they left the game. There was no **Social Security** to help and no **pension** money from baseball. In the 1920s, Major League Baseball realized that a number of old players like Lou badly needed help, so the teams started to raise money and held games for charity.

A large crowd attended the game in Boston, which meant there was money to send to those who needed it. It is safe to say that Cy would not have missed playing in that game for just about any reason. His friend Lou needed help, and Cy was there to do what he could.

If he couldn't make it to the ballpark, Cy could listen to a game on radio. In the early 1920s, radio stations had begun broadcasting ball games so that fans who lived far away from their hometowns or could not get to the park had a chance to hear the entire game. Cy could hear the Indians broadcasts from Cleveland and likely the Pirates games from Pittsburgh. Before television began in the 1940s, the best way to follow Major League Baseball was on the radio and in the newspapers. Fans listened to the games and the next morning picked up the paper to read the box scores from other games around the country. By the 1950s there were millions of television sets around the United States. Cy never talked about it, but he lived long enough to hear the first games on radio and later to see at least a few ball games on TV.

In summer 1932, Cy received an invitation to the opening of a large new stadium in Cleveland. When League Park had been built in 1891, 9,000 seats were enough for the Spiders fans. As the years passed, more people moved to Cleveland, and a much larger ballpark was needed. A new stadium was built downtown, right off Lake Erie. The new place would be able to seat as many as 79,000 people!

On July 31, 1932, Cleveland Municipal Stadium opened for baseball. The Cleveland team owners brought many former players from the Spiders and Naps to stand on the field and let the fans see them one more time. Cy stood in line with Chief Zimmer, his old catcher from forty years earlier. The newspapers took photos of the players, and it was a grand time for the baseball fans in Cleveland.

Cy was a having a great retirement, spending time with Bobby and friends and visiting many ballparks in both leagues. He was healthy and looked forward to the years ahead. Though all seemed to be going well, in late January 1934, Bobby became sick. Cy watched over her, but she did not get better and needed to be taken to Union Hospital. The doctors did everything they could, but after a week of care, Bobby passed away at age sixty-one. Cy had loved his wife ever since they were schoolkids and through forty-two years of marriage. They were best friends who depended on each other. They had no children, leaving Cy alone in his house and farm.

As the days went by, Cy grew lonely in the empty house. He missed working outside and coming home to Bobby. Soon, he decided that living alone was too hard for him, and he sold all his land, including the house. He moved in with his neighbors, John and Ruth Benedum, and helped them with their smaller farm. He got up every morning at

6:00, ate his favorite breakfast of pancakes, sausage, and coffee, then headed outside to begin his chores. Cy fed the animals, including his favorite cow Bessie, cleaned out the barn, and chopped some wood. He worked until late afternoon, had dinner, and went to bed by 9:00.

Cy had been living with the Benedums for a short time when Ruth gave birth to a daughter, whom they named Jane. From the beginning, Cy acted as Jane's grandfather, holding her in his lap, warming her bottle, and probably changing a few diapers. Taking care of little Jane helped Cy get over his loneliness after Bobby died.

While holding two jobs, one as a farmworker and the other as a grandpa, Cy learned of some exciting news from Major League Baseball. The league was planning to build a Hall of Fame in Cooperstown, New York, to be opened in June 1939. A lot of people close to the game believed that baseball had started right there in the small village of Cooperstown, invented by a man named Abner Doubleday. With that in mind, baseball picked the village as the place for the National Baseball Hall of Fame. The vote to decide the first players to be named to the Hall of Fame was held in 1936. The Baseball Writers Association of America was to do all the voting, and a player needed 75 percent of the votes to be elected. The writers were to choose from players who had played in the major leagues since 1900. That covered thirty-six years and thousands of ballplayers.

In the first election, the writers' association picked five players: two pitchers, Walter Johnson and Christy Mathewson; one infielder, Honus Wagner; and two outfielders, Ty Cobb and Babe Ruth. Yes, it is true—Cy did not make the Hall of Fame in the first election. It is hard to guess why that happened, but Cy had played almost half of his career before 1900, and that may have been on the minds of the voters.

One year later, on January 19, 1937, Cy received 151 votes out of 201, which equaled 75 percent and a place in the Hall of Fame. Only three former players got in that year, including Cy. The other two were both from Cleveland: Nap Lajoie and Tris Speaker, the player-manager of the 1920 world champion Indians.

Benedum home, 2018.
Courtesy of the Newcomerstown Historical Society, Newcomerstown, Ohio

In early May 1937, Cy told sportswriters he was going to donate his trophies and awards to the Hall of Fame. It was a great thing to do because the new museum needed items to fill its displays. People coming from all parts of the United States could see the loving cups that Cy had received in Boston in 1908 or the bats and gloves used by Babe Ruth and Ty Cobb. Cy was one of the first to be so generous in offering his trophies to Cooperstown.

Two years later, the big day came. Cy, Nap Lajoie, and Tris Speaker all traveled to Cooperstown in June 1939 to be part of the opening ceremonies of the newly completed National Baseball Hall of Fame. Cy, now seventy-two years old, stood outside the Hall of Fame with Honus Wagner, Walter Johnson, Babe Ruth, and all the others. There were speeches by the mayor of Cooperstown and by the two presidents of Major League Baseball. Then it was time to hear from the new members. Each gave a short speech to the 4,000 fans gathered outside the building on Main Street. Cy got a big hand from the crowd when he said, "I hope baseball climbs to even greater success in the next 100 years than it had in the first 100!"[1]

Cy's trophies from his long career. They are now in the National Baseball Hall of Fame and Museum, Cooperstown, New York.

Courtesy of the Newcomerstown Historical Society, Newcomerstown, Ohio

After the ceremony, Cy and the other Hall of Fame members put on their old uniforms and marched to Doubleday Field for a game between two teams made up of current American and National League ballplayers. Just the way children did on playgrounds and ball fields everywhere, the team captains took turns picking players until all were taken. A giant crowd of 10,000 fans watched their favorite stars play seven innings until it was time for everyone to catch their trains home. It must have been a perfect day for Cy, with the happy memories he would keep for the rest of his life.

Back home in Peoli, Cy kept to his farm chores and taking care of little Jane Benedum. He already had a full life as a baseball player, Hall of Fame member, and farmer. What more could there be for him? Well, in 1947, the people of Newcomerstown met to talk about a big party for Cy's eightieth birthday. It would take up an entire day with lots of homemade food, a big birthday cake, a special dinner, presents, and a speech or two from Cy's friends. The date was set for March 29, with former major league pitchers Waite Hoyt and Sam Jones attending along with Bill Veeck, the owner of the Cleveland Indians.

At 10:30 a.m., all the downtown stores placed large signs in their windows that read "Happy Birthday Cy!" Shortly after, Cy arrived in Newcomerstown to sit down at a special table and sign a few hundred autographs. Cy patiently signed each baseball and photo handed to him until all the people in line had gotten his autograph. He then went to the Elks Club, where Waite Hoyt, Sam Jones, and Pat Donahue, a backup catcher for the 1908 Boston team, waited for him. The old ballplayers talked until lunch, when they walked back downtown for a concert by the Newcomerstown High School band.

After the music, Cy took a rest at a friend's house until dinner. There were so many people attending the evening event that it had to be held at five different places all around Newcomerstown. Where Cy ate his roast beef dinner, there was a birthday cake five feet high with three layers and eighty roses in honor of him! After everybody finished eating, there was a program in the auditorium led by the governor of Ohio, who read telegrams from former players around the United States.

Bill Veeck came to the microphone and gave Cy the keys to a shiny new automobile. Mr. Veeck had Cy sign a contract to pitch again for the 1947 Cleveland Indians. It was all in fun, as Cy smiled and signed. Later the mayor gave Cy the key to the city, and a group of friends brought him 2,803 pennies for all the strikeouts during his career.

Cy was grateful for the new auto, but his eyes were weakening, and it became too hard for him to drive to Cleveland and other cities. The state police came up with the idea of giving a special license to fourteen-year-old Jane Benedum to allow her to drive Cy's car anywhere in Ohio. Jane became Cy's personal driver, taking him to Cleveland and back for baseball games and visits.

Around this time, Cy became interested in Little League Baseball. The program began in Pennsylvania but had spread to Ohio and many other states. Cy liked to watch the children play ball and to give advice. Parents and kids always listened closely to what Cy had to say. Later, Cy would attend the Little League World Series in Williamsport, Pennsylvania, and at one game threw out the first pitch. Cy believed that young people were the future and that learning baseball would help them understand the importance of teamwork and playing by the rules.

Though Cy was well past his eightieth birthday, he kept busy answering letters, going to baseball games, and working on the farm. He told reporters that he no longer got up at 6:00 a.m., but still chopped wood and fed the animals. In 1955, Cy once again was a guest at the Little League World Series. Even though he was by then eighty-eight years old, he stood on the pitcher's mound and threw a strike to the catcher.

In late October 1955, Cy had trouble breathing and felt pain in his chest. A doctor came to see him and thought he should be taken to Union Hospital. But before they could get him there, Cy passed away on November 5, while sleeping quietly in his favorite chair. His heart, which had been strong for so many years, just stopped beating. Funeral plans were made for Monday, November 7, at the Peoli Church.

On the morning of the funeral, hundreds of people crowded into the small, red-brick church. The reverend leading the service said about Cy, "Young's memory will live on forever. A green farm boy from the hills of Tuscarawas County has returned to the land he loved."[2]

After the funeral, the guests walked to the top of the hill behind the church where Cy was to be buried. From that spot, the view extended far down to the valley, almost to where Cy had been born. Many ballplayers were there for the burial, including Bob Feller, Tris Speaker, and Steve O'Neill, who played for Cleveland's 1920 World Series champs.

Cy was buried next to Bobby, with a large stone monument telling about his baseball career. In later years, people visiting the grave would leave baseballs and bats in front of the stone. People will never forget Cy Young and everything he did in his baseball career.

Cy and Bobby's headstone, 2018. Note the spelling here of "Roba." All other sources use "Robba."

Courtesy of the Newcomerstown Historical Society, Newcomerstown, Ohio

A year after Cy had passed away, Ford Frick, the commissioner of baseball, had a great idea. He met with all the team owners and asked them to approve an award for the best pitcher in baseball each year and to name it in honor of Cy Young. The owners agreed, and the Cy Young Award was born. Ten years later, it was decided that the award should be given to the best pitcher in each league. Many of the greatest hurlers in baseball have received the Cy Young Award, including Sandy Koufax, Bob Gibson, Randy Johnson, and Roger Clemens.

In 1993, thirty-eight years after Cy died, he received another honor. In Boston, a large bronze statue was erected near the spot where Cy started the first game of the 1903 World Series. Huntington Avenue Grounds had been torn down many years before, and in its place was the campus of Northeastern University. The statue stands six feet, eight inches tall and weighs a thousand pounds. Cy is there in his Boston Americans uniform, leaning toward home plate with his right hand behind his back holding the baseball. He looks as though, in a moment, he is about to throw that fastball to the thousands of batters who swung and hit nothing but the air.

DID YOU KNOW?

Every June, Newcomerstown, Ohio, holds Cy Young Days. The celebration features food, games, music, and old-time baseball played during the weekend. A Cy Young Award winner is invited each year to attend the three-day event.

Cy's Timeline

April 1865
> The American Civil War ends. McKinzie Young Jr. returns home to Ohio.

March 29, 1867
> Denton True Young is born in Gilmore, Ohio.

1885
> Denton moves to Red Cloud, Nebraska. Pitches for local team.

April 30, 1890
> Denton pitches his first professional game for Canton.

August 1890
> Denton is sold to the Cleveland Spiders of the National League.

August 6, 1890
> Denton wins his first National League game, 8–1 over Chicago.

September 1890
> Newspapers start to call Denton "Cyclone" or "Cy" because of how fast he can throw.

October 1890
> Cy pitches and wins both games of a doubleheader.

May 1, 1891
> Cleveland's League Park opens. Cy pitches and wins, 12–3.

October 1892
> Cy finishes the season with thirty-six wins, the best in the National League.

November 8, 1892
> Cy marries Robba Miller. He calls her "Bobby."

October 1893
> The Youngs visit the Chicago World's Fair.

October 1895

The Spiders win the Temple Cup against Baltimore. Cy wins three games.

September 18, 1897

Cy pitches his first no-hitter, winning 6–0 over Cincinnati.

March 1899

Frank Robison buys the St. Louis team. Cy is sent there from Cleveland.

March 1901

The American League begins. Cy leaves St. Louis for the Boston Americans.

June 1901

Cy starts twelve-game winning streak.

October 1901

Cy leads the American League with 33 wins and 158 strikeouts.

October 1, 1903

The first-ever World Series game takes place in Boston. Cy loses, 7–3.

October 7, 1903

Cy gets his first win in a World Series game, beating Pittsburgh, 5–3. Boston goes on to win the series.

April 1904

Cy begins a streak of forty-five innings pitched without allowing a run.

May 5, 1904

Cy pitches a perfect game, the first in Major League Baseball since 1880.

June 30, 1908

Cy pitches his third no-hitter at age forty-one, the oldest to do it. His record will stand until 1990.

August 13, 1908

Cy Young Day is held at Huntington Avenue Grounds, Boston. Cy receives $7,000 from the Boston owner.

February 1909

Boston trades Cy to Cleveland for two players and cash.

July 19, 1910

Cy wins his 500th game, against Washington.

August 1911

Cleveland gives Cy his release. He signs a new contract with Boston of the National League.

October 6, 1911

Cy pitches his last game in the Major Leagues. He loses, 13–3.

August 1912

Cy officially retires from baseball at age forty-five.

July 31, 1932

Municipal Stadium in Cleveland opens. Cy is invited to the game and brought onto the field.

January 25, 1934

Robba "Bobby" Young dies at age sixty-three.

January 19, 1937

Cy is elected to the National Baseball Hall of Fame.

June 12, 1939

Cy is inducted into the National Baseball Hall of Fame at the opening ceremony.

March 29, 1947

A huge party takes place in Newcomerstown for Cy's eightieth birthday. Cy is given a new car.

November 5, 1955

Cy Young dies at age eighty-eight.

November 7, 1955

Cy's funeral is held in Peoli. Over 300 people attend, including Major League Baseball players.

March 1956

The Cy Young Award is started, to be given each year to the best pitcher in baseball.

September 1993

A statue of Cy is placed on the Northeastern University campus in Boston on the site of the first-ever World Series game, which Cy pitched.

Glossary

appendicitis: when the appendix, a small tube near the intestines, becomes infected and causes great pain

ball: a pitch that is outside the strike zone

bootblack: a person who shines boots or shoes

bottom half (of inning): when the home team comes to bat

brass band: a musical group that consists mainly of brass instruments like tubas, trombones, and trumpets

champagne: a type of expensive bubbly wine, made from grapes

contract: a written agreement between two people; in baseball the player agrees to play for a certain amount of money

crank: an old term for a baseball fan

creamery: a business that purifies milk and butter and sells them to stores

curveball: a pitch that moves at an angle to the left or right of home plate

double: when a batter hits the ball safely and is able to advance to second base

doubleheader: when two teams play two games in a single day

earned run average (ERA): the average number of runs a pitcher gives up per game; the ERA is nine times earned runs divided by innings pitched

error: when a fielder drops a fly ball or misses an easy ground ball and the batter reaches first base

feat: an impressive achievement

fielder: any of nine players on the baseball field who try to catch a batted ball and stop the batter or hitter from getting on base

fixing: when a player does not perform well on purpose in order for his team to lose, usually in exchange for money from gamblers betting that the team will lose the game

forfeit: when a team does not have enough players or is too late to play a game, the other team is declared the winner

foul ball: a ball batted outside the lines that mark the edge of the field

free agent: a ballplayer who does not have a contract with any team and has the right to choose where to play

general admission: a low-priced ticket to a game where the seat is not reserved

grandstand: where fans sit inside a ballpark in seats or on benches

ground ball: a batted ball that stays on the ground; it is either picked up by an infielder or reaches the outfield for a hit

hayseed: a term used to make fun of someone from a farm or small town

hit: the act of a batter making contact with the baseball and reaching any base safely

home plate: the spot on the infield that the batter stands next to and the catcher crouches behind; the pitcher tries to throw the baseball over home plate without the batter hitting it

infield: the area that contains home plate and the three bases where the first, second, and third baseman and the shortstop, catcher, and pitcher play

inning: there are nine innings to a complete baseball game (unless the game goes into extra innings when the score is tied after the ninth inning); both teams bat each inning until three outs are made per team

line drive: a hard-hit ball that travels through the air in a nearly straight line, usually low to the ground, rather than being popped up high in the air

loaded the bases: the team at bat has runners on all three bases

loving cup: a large container usually made of silver and given to the winners of a game or contest

luxury box: a special seat at a game that is more comfortable than general admission

malaria: a serious and sometimes fatal disease carried by mosquitoes

megaphone: a large horn that makes the voice louder when spoken through, like a microphone or loudspeaker

newsboy: a young boy who sells newspapers out on the street

no-hitter: when a pitcher throws a complete game without allowing a hit

out: when a batter fails to reach a base safely

outfield: the large space beyond the infield where the left, center, and right fielder play

pennant: a banner indicating that a baseball team finished in first place

pension: an amount of money given monthly to people from their job when retired

perfect game: a game in which the pitcher never allows a single batter to get on base

pinch hitter: when a ballplayer is sent into a game to bat in place of another

pitcher's box: an area four feet by five and a half feet where the pitcher stands when throwing the baseball to home plate

pitcher's mound: an artificial low hill on which the pitcher stands

rival: an opponent or challenger

rooter: an early term for a baseball fan

safe: if the runner gets to the base before the ball or before being tagged

saloon: a bar, a place serving alcohol

scorecard: a small booklet bought at the ballpark that lists the players and has a page for keeping score

semipro: to play baseball once or twice a week and get paid a small amount each game

shaking off: when a pitcher does not like the pitch his catcher has signaled or called for and shakes his head to ask for another pitch

shirk: to avoid doing a job or task

shortstop: the fielder stationed between second and third bases

shutout: when a pitcher does not allow a single run to score in a game

single: when a batter hits the ball safely and is able to reach first base

Social Security: money set aside by the government to be used in retirement

starting lineup: the players named by the manager to play in a certain game

steal: when a runner has successfully advanced to the next base without a batted ball or a walk

streetcar: a type of bus that was powered by electricity in overhead wires; each streetcar had a pole that attached to the wires and moved it along

strike: a pitch that is in the strike zone *or* a swing and a miss by the batter

strikeout: when a batter has three strikes thrown by the pitcher and is out

strike zone: an area the width of home plate and the height between a batter's armpits and knees

telegram: a message received from a telegraph

telegraph: an electric device sending messages over wires for long distances

ticket window: where to buy tickets for an event

tonsillitis: when the tissues (tonsils) in your throat get infected

top half (of inning): the time when the visiting team comes to bat

triple: when a batter hits the ball safely and is able to advance to third base

tuberculosis: a disease that destroys your lungs and in Cy's time usually caused death

turnstile: a gate that allows only one person at a time to pass through

walk: when a pitcher throws four balls outside the strike zone and the batter does not swing at any of them, the batter automatically goes to first base

windup: how a pitcher gets into position to throw the ball

win-loss record: the number of games won compared to the number of games lost

Acknowledgments

I want to extend my sincere thanks to the wonderful staff at Ohio University Press for all their support over the last few years. It was not easy to make the transition from writing for adults to writing for children, but the editors at Ohio University made the task painless and enjoyable. Thanks to the Newcomerstown Historical Society and Newcomerstown Library for their help in doing research and getting me to Peoli without being lost. Many thanks to the National Baseball Hall of Fame Library in Cooperstown for providing the player files and rare photos.

In completing this project, I must give thanks to my patient wife, Vicki, who provided enough support for three or four books and let me spend countless hours writing and rewriting without a complaint. I owe you much love and at least several movies and a long vacation. And to my two great-nephews whom I love dearly, Carson and Mason, I hope in about seven or eight years this work will have some meaning for you.

Notes

Chapter 1. In the Beginning

1. Franklin Lewis, *The Cleveland Indians* (New York: Putnam, 1949), 22.
2. Cy Young Player File, National Baseball Hall of Fame Library.

Chapter 2. The Pride of the Spiders

1. *Canton Repository*, July 26, 1890.
2. Cy Young Player File, National Baseball Hall of Fame Library.
3. *Cleveland Plain Dealer*, August 10, 1890, 7.

Chapter 3. League Park Opens

1. *Cleveland Leader*, May 2, 1891, 3.
2. *Cleveland Leader*, April 1, 1892, 3.
3. *Cleveland Leader*, July 3, 1892, 15.

Chapter 5. The Temple Cup

1. *Cleveland Plain Dealer*, July 17, 1895, 5.
2. *New York Mercury*, August 20, 1895.
3. Jerry Lansche, *Glory Fades Away* (Dallas: Taylor Publishing, 1991), 243–44, 248, 255.
4. David Voight, *American Baseball* (Pennsylvania: Penn State University Press, 1983), 253–55.
5. *Cleveland Plain Dealer*, October 3, 1895, 2.

Chapter 6. Cy Changes Teams

1. Lou Criger Family Papers.
2. *St. Louis Post-Dispatch*, August 25, 1899, 5.
3. *Sporting Life*, March 1901.
4. *Denver Post*, April 4 1901, 10.
5. *Denver Post*, April 4, 1901, 10.
6. *Pawtucket (RI) Times*, March 29, 1901, 2.

Chapter 7. The World Series Begins

1. *Cleveland Plain Dealer*, May 28, 1901, 8.
2. *Boston Herald*, February 19, 1902.
3. *Boston Journal*, February 22, 1902.
4. *Mansfield (OH) News Journal*, March 25, 1903.
5. Cy Young Player File, National Baseball Hall of Fame, Lou Criger Family Papers.
6. Lawrence Ritter, *The Glory of Their Times* (New York: Macmillan, 1966), 27.
7. *Boston Journal*, October 14, 1903, 8.

Chapter 8. Cy Is Perfect

1. *Cincinnati Post*, November 4, 1903, 4.
2. *Cleveland Plain Dealer*, May 8, 1904, 35.
3. *Boston Journal*, May 6, 1904, 1.
4. *Cleveland Plain Dealer*, March 19, 1905, 26.
5. Lou Criger Player File, National Baseball Hall of Fame.
6. *Cleveland Plain Dealer*, January 12, 1909, 9.
7. *Cleveland Plain Dealer*, February 17, 1909, 1.

Chapter 9. A New Record

1. *East Liverpool (OH) Evening Review*, October 22, 1910, 14.
2. *Cleveland Plain Dealer*, April 15, 1911, 14.
3. *Cleveland Plain Dealer*, August 16, 1911, 1.

Chapter 10. The Hall of Fame Calls

1. *Cleveland Plain Dealer,* June 13, 1939, 16.
2. *Canton Repository,* November 8, 1955, 12.

Bibliography

Books

Benson, Michael. *Ballparks of North America.* Jefferson, NC: McFarland, 1989.

Browning, Reed. *Cy Young: A Baseball Life.* Amherst: University of Massachusetts Press, 2003.

Cobb, Ty. *Memoirs of Twenty Years in Baseball.* Edited by William R. Cobb. Marietta, GA: William R. Cobb, 2002.

Lansche, Jerry. *Glory Fades Away: The Nineteenth-Century World Series Rediscovered.* Dallas: Taylor Publishing, 1991.

Ritter, Lawrence. *The Glory of Their Times: The Story of the Early Days of Baseball Told by the Men Who Played It.* New York: Macmillan, 1966.

Romig, Ralph H. *Cy Young: Baseball's Legendary Giant.* Philadelphia: Dorrance, 1964; repr., N.p.: Ohio Hills, 1983.

Newspapers and Magazines

Cleveland Leader (1891–1905)

Cleveland Plain Dealer (1890–1939)

Newcomerstown News (1890–1911)

Sporting Life (1896–1904)

Libraries and Archives

National Baseball Hall of Fame and Museum, Cooperstown, New York (player files Denton "Cy" Young, Lou Criger, Charles "Chief" Zimmer, Oliver Wendell "Patsy" Tebeau)

Newcomerstown Public Library, Newcomerstown, Ohio

Newcomerstown Historical Society, Newcomerstown, Ohio (Cy Young Collection)
Webster County Historical Museum, Red Cloud, Nebraska

Personal Correspondence

Lou Criger Family

Biographies for Young Readers